Books by Harvey Frommer

BASEBALL'S GREATEST RIVALRY:
THE NEW YORK YANKEES AND BOSTON RED SOX

RICKEY AND ROBINSON

BASKETBALL MY WAY
(*by Nancy Lieberman with Myrna Frommer*)

THE SPORTS DATE BOOK
(*with Myrna Frommer*)

NEW YORK CITY BASEBALL: 1947–1957

THE GREAT AMERICAN SOCCER BOOK

SPORTS ROOTS

SPORTS LINGO

THE MARTIAL ARTS: JUDO AND KARATE

A SAILING PRIMER
(*with Ron Weinmann*)

A BASEBALL CENTURY

BASEBALL'S GREATEST RIVALRY:

The New York Yankees and Boston Red Sox

BASEBALL'S GREATEST RIVALRY:

The New York Yankees

and

Boston Red Sox

HARVEY FROMMER

Atheneum 1982 *New York*

Library of Congress Cataloging in Publication Data

Frommer, Harvey.
  Baseball's greatest rivalry.
  1. New York Yankees (Baseball team)—History.
  2. Boston Red Sox (Baseball team)—History. I. Title.
GV875.N45F67 1982   796.357′64′097471   81–69159
  ISBN 0-689-11270-X   AACR2

Published simultaneously in Canada by McClelland and Stewart Ltd.
Composition by American-Stratford Graphic Services,
Brattleboro, Vermont
Manufactured by Fairfield Graphics,
Fairfield, Pennsylvania
First Edition

For my son, FREDDY,
who made a great catch
of a ball hit by Johnny Pesky
at Fenway Park, September 6, 1981

ACKNOWLEDGMENTS

Writing a book for me is always an enjoyable experience. Most of the time a great deal of that joy comes through contact with people who are kind enough to give up their time, their memories and their insights. All the individuals and organizations listed—no matter which side of the rivalry they were on—were of great help to me. I would like to extend my sincere thanks to Larry Sheehan (my editor at Atheneum), Marvin Brown (of Atheneum), Bill Crowley, Lou Piniella, Mike Torrez, Mickey Mantle, Irv Kaze, Johnny Pesky, Phil Rizzuto, Hawk Harrelson, Charlie Lau, Frank Messer, Bob Watson, Ralph Houk,

Acknowledgments

Eddie Yost, Dwight Evans, Til Ferdenzi, Phil Pepe, Mike Geffner, Ron Luciano, Bob Fishel, Clifford Kachline, Wynn Bates, Chico Walker, David Szen, James Bontakis.

Also, the Boston Red Sox, the New York Yankees, the American League, the Baseball Hall of Fame and its staff at Cooperstown, New York.

And the team on the bench—Granny, Caroline, Jennifer, Freddy, Ian.

The largest debt and thank you is for Myrna, my wife. Her organizational skills and language facility ease all my writing efforts.

H.F.

CONTENTS

ix

ILLUSTRATIONS

BASEBALL'S GREATEST RIVALRY:

The New York Yankees and Boston Red Sox

COLLISION

In 1976 the New York Yankees finished the season with a
97–62 record and won the American League East title.
The Red Sox of Boston finished in third place, 15½ games
behind. In 1977, the Yankees won 100 of the 162 games
they played and repeated as division title winners. Boston
won 97 games and tied for second place with Baltimore.
Both teams trailed the Yankees by 2½ games.

It was during these two seasons that more and more
Yankee fans began to sport "Red Sox Suck" tee shirts.
And it was during this time that Yankee principal owner
George Steinbrenner kept wheeling and dealing, embel-

lishing the Yankee image—his team's skills and the Red Sox failings.

The start of the 1978 season gave Boston fans hope. Over the winter the team had made some key moves to strengthen itself. Mike Torrez, winner of two World Series games for the Yankees in 1977, was signed as a free agent. Dennis Eckersley, just 23, was acquired from the Cleveland Indians. It was felt that the combination of the veteran Torrez and the youthful Eckersley would shore up Sox pitching. Another key Boston acquisition was Jerry Remy, a sure-handed, speedy second baseman obtained from the California Angels. Remy's promise was added speed on the basepaths and an effective contact hitter near the top of the Boston batting order.

With Remy at second base and Rick Burleson at shortstop, Boston fans felt their team had a double-play combination to rival if not surpass the Yankee tandem of Bucky Dent and Willie Randolph. George Scott, the Sox first baseman, had recorded 33 homers in 1977—almost twice the total of Yankee first baseman Chris Chambliss. Slugging Butch Hobson was a fixture at third base. Nettles of New York was peerless with a glove, but Sox fans argued that Hobson outmatched the Yankee third baseman when it came to hitting. Hobson had rapped 30 homers and driven in 112 runs in 1977.

Both teams boasted top-flight catchers. Most baseball experts rated Boston's Carlton Fisk and New York's Thurman Munson among the two best backstops in all of baseball.

Both teams had powerful, clutch-hitting outfield performers, capable of making crucial defensive plays. Carl Yastrzemski, Dwight Evans and Fred Lynn would be

"Louisiana Lightning"—Ron Guidry—who proved that great southpaws could win at Fenway

Boston's picket line, augmented by perhaps the best potential designated hitter in all of baseball—Jim Rice. The Yankees had steady Roy White, flamboyant Mickey Rivers, and dramatic Reggie Jackson, buttressed by Paul Blair, Lou Piniella and, if needed, Cliff Johnson.

If there was a key difference, it was in pitching. Over the winter Steinbrenner had signed Rich Gossage, Rawly Eastwick and Andy Messersmith. This trio joined Catfish Hunter, Don Gullett, Sparky Lyle, Ed Figueroa, Ken Holtzman, Dick Tidrow and Ron Guidry (16–7 in 1977 and getting better, much better).

Against this array of all types of pitching talent, Boston had its Latin duo of Luis Tiant and Mike Torrez, Eckersley, Bill Lee and Bob Stanley. Bill Campbell had saved 31 games in 1977 and it was felt that he could repeat that performance in 1978.

Seven straight wins at Fenway Park launched Boston on a fine start as the season got underway. By May 18 the Yankees (19–13) trailed the second-place Sox (23–12), who were a half-game behind the surprising first-place Detroit Tigers. On May 24 the Sox moved into undisputed possession of first place. They would remain there for 113 days, to the delight of their adoring and rabid fans. At the All-Star break, powered by a combination of good pitching and power hitting, Boston had racked up a record of 57 wins against just 26 losses—the best record in all of baseball. More enjoyable to Red Sox fans was the record of the New York Yankees. The New Yorkers were mired in third place, 11½ games out.

Emanating daily from New York was news of controversy, sore-armed pitchers, bruised infielders, battered egos, unhappy coaches. In Boston, for a change, there was relative harmony.

On July 18, the Sox stretched their lead over the Yanks to 14 games. "Even Affirmed couldn't catch the Red Sox now," snapped Reggie Jackson, referring to the horse that had won the 1978 Triple Crown.

Off the field Yankee activity was more explosive than anything they were doing on the field. Dissension prevailed. Sparky Lyle was fined $500 for taking himself out of a game, but the fine was later dropped. Reggie Jackson was suspended "indefinitely" on July 17 for refusing to bunt in a game against Kansas City. Jackson struck out—and this, rather than the bunt refusal, instigated the suspension levied by manager Billy Martin that lasted five days. It was reported that Steinbrenner ordered Martin to reinstate Jackson to the lineup. A piqued, infuriated, frazzled Martin delivered a long monologue to reporters. The phrase that received the most publicity was "The two of them [Jackson and Steinbrenner] deserve each other. One's a born liar, the other's convicted."

One day after his outburst, Martin bowed out as Yankee manager. He was replaced by Bob Lemon, who just a few weeks before had been sacked as Chicago White Sox pilot. The low-keyed Lemon proved a dramatic counterpoint to the hyperactive Martin. With the Hall of Fame pitcher managing mildly and carefully, the Yankees started to move. Boston, battered by injuries, started to fade. With Rick Burleson and Carl Yastrzemski sidelined with physical ailments, with Mike Torrez and Bill Lee suddenly ineffective, the Sox saw their lead drop to 7½ games on July 30. Lee, 7–0 at one point, couldn't buy a win. His downward spiral continued throughout the sea-

son, which he finished with a 10–10 record and a 3.46
ERA.

On August 3 the Yanks and Sox met in a two-game series. Boston's lead had skidded to 6½ games. New York
had won 12 of its last 16 contests, while Boston had been
victorious in just three out of its last 14. To the delight of
their fans, the Sox swept the Yanks, 7–5 and 8–1, and increased their lead to 8½ games. It was a Pyrrhic victory.
The double loss seemed only to motivate the Yanks more.

Down through the humid weeks of August, in the hot
sun of the day and through the cool breezes of evening,
the two teams played out their strange seasons. "The 1978
season was like two seasons in one," notes Phil Pepe, who
has been covering the Yankees regularly for the New
York *Daily News* since 1971. "The Sox had made just two
roster changes in the first half of the season; the Yankees
had all kinds of physical problems. The second half of the
season was just the reverse."

Catfish Hunter, who had slumped, suddenly regained
his pitching rhythm. Bucky Dent, who had been sidelined
with injuries for almost a month, was well again. Reggie
Jackson, enraged and driven, began to take out his fury
on opposing pitchers. On August 10 he went on a tear
that saw him pound 13 homers, drive in 49 runs and
notch a .288 batting average.

For Boston the season continued in a downhill slide.
Steady Jerry Remy chipped a bone in his left wrist on
August 25. Sox fans groaned at the prognosis: "Quick return doubtful." Five days later Dwight Evans was
beaned. He would not be the same again in 1978.

As the season turned into September, it was almost as if
the first-place Sox were chasing the second-place Yan-

kees. On the seventh day of September, Boston's lead was just four games over the charging Yankees as the rivals prepared for a four-game series at Fenway Park. Boston had played 25–24 ball since its July 24 14-game lead. New York had won 35 of 49 games in the same timespan. Writers billed the Yankee drive as the "Great Comeback"; Boston's behavior was called the "Great Collapse." Red Sox fans clamoring for tickets, hovering around their TV sets and radios, had earthier expressions. "Before the series got underway, the managers were talked to by the umpires," notes former American League umpire Ron Luciano. "Throughout 1978, the entire Boston–New York series was handled like a play-off because of the history of bad blood between the teams."

Mike Torrez opposed his former Yankee teammates in the first game; Catfish Hunter started for the New Yorkers. Torrez didn't have it. He was touched for two tallies in the first inning as Munson and Jackson both padded their RBI records. In the second inning, Torrez was lashed for four straight singles and left the game muttering to himself. The handsome right-hander's last victory had been on August 18. After two innings, the score was 5–0, Yankees. After three innings, the score was 7–0, Yankees. After four innings, it was 12–0, Yankees. A Boston reporter quipped, "There was a traffic jam outside of Fenway as fans fought with each other trying to get home in time for *Hawaii Five-O*."

The standing-room-only crowd at Fenway was shocked and sour. They could not believe the mauling their favorites were experiencing. When the debacle finally ended, the Yankees had a 15–3 triumph. They had treated their fans to a fireworks display of their offensive might by cracking out 20 hits to all parts of the little ballpark. It was a humbling experience for the Sox and their fans. There was more to come, and soon.

Rookie Jim Wright (8–4 in 1978) opposed Yankee rookie pitcher Jim Beattie (6–9 in 1978). The pounding inflicted on the Sox by the Yanks the day before was immediately evident.

The Hub players were tentative while the team from the Big Apple was tenaciously aggressive. Mickey Rivers led off the game with a single, stole second, moved to third on a Fisk throwing error. The Yanks led 2–0 after one inning and then opened up their offensive engine full throttle in the second.

A Lou Piniella triple and a Roy White single scored one Yankee run. White swiped second and wound up on third base as Fisk committed another throwing flub. Dent brought White home with a sacrifice fly for the Yank's second run of the inning. Tom Burgmeier replaced Wright on the mound for the Sox. Rivers rapped out another single. Munson drew a base on balls. And then Reggie Jackson smashed a home run to score three more runs. Chris Chambliss singled. Burgmeier mishandled a bunt by Nettles. Piniella slashed his second extra base hit of the inning—a double that scored the Yankee's sixth run in the second and increased their lead to 8–0. The game's final score was 13–2, Yankees.

In two games, Boston had committed nine errors. So unsteady were the Sox that they had actually committed 23 errors in their last nine games, to yield 19 unearned runs. The Yanks had pounded out 28 runs to Boston's five and had outhit the Sox, 38–14.

"I can't believe this is happening," said Yankee super-scout Clyde King. "I could understand it if an expansion team fell apart like this, but Boston's got the best record in all of baseball. It can't go on like this."

A shaken Boston press reacted with jibes against the BoSox. "If you need directions to home plate at Fenway Park," proclaimed a *Boston Globe* story, "just stop and ask any New York Yankee. They've all been there already."

Boston manager Don Zimmer tabbed Dennis Eckersly to pitch the third game of the series, on September 9. Bob Lemon, confident but not complacent, chose Ron Guidry. The Sox were staggering but they were playing on their own home ground and Lemon went out of his way to point out how, while pitching for Cleveland, he once was leading 11–1 at Fenway and wound up losing the game.

Eckersley was the best pitcher the beleaguered Zimmer could call on. His record was 16–6, and he was unbeaten in nine decisions at Fenway. But Guidry was the best pitcher in all of baseball—he boasted a glittering 20–2 record, a popping fastball and a dancing slider.

There were 33,611 people at the park, most of them Sox zealots. The Yankees did not score in the top of the first inning and the huge crowd sounded off with a mock roar of approval for Eckersley's effort.

Rick Burleson singled to center to lead things off for Boston. His line drive buzzed perilously close to Guidry's head. Fred Lynn laid down a sacrifice bunt that moved Burleson to second. Jim Rice came up to hit. The roaring Red Sox rooters screamed out encouragement. Rice swung but was out in front of the ball and grounded to short. In the hole, Dent had trouble getting a handle on the ball, and Rice beat the throw to first. Yaz faced

Guidry. With the runners leading off the corners and just one out, it seemed the Sox had the "Ragin Cajun" on the ropes, but Yaz grounded out weakly and Fisk was called out on strikes to end the inning.

It was not only the end of the inning, it was also the end of the Red Sox chances for victory that day. Guidry did not allow another hit. Eckersley matched the Yankee pitcher until the fourth inning.

Then Thurman Munson popped a single to right field to open things up for the Yanks. Jackson smacked the ball to the left-field corner. Yaz chased it down and fired in a fine relay throw to second baseman Frank Duffy who pegged the ball to Scott at first base to double Munson. Streamers, scorecards, whistles and waving Red Sox caps vied with each other as the Fens rolled with joy at the heroics of the suddenly rejuvenated defense.

A Chris Chambliss double quieted things down. With two on and two out, Nettles was intentionally walked, as Zimmer elected to pitch to Piniella. The embattled BoSox skipper later would be severely second-guessed. Piniella was the only Yankee batting over .300, and in the clutch he was a deadly professional performer.

Lou lofted a short fly to right-center field. Five Boston players gave chase. The wind played with the ball and it dropped in. Chambliss scored. Nettles moved to third and Piniella was elated on second base with his gift pop-fly double. Roy White was intentionally passed to load the bases. With a 1–2 count, Dent kicked at the dirt and readied himself for Eckersley's fourth pitch—a high fastball. Dent slammed it to left. Nettles scored. Piniella scored. White wound up on third and Dent cruised into second base as Yaz mishandled the ball. "It was that hit," Eckersley groaned, "that broke my back."

Roy White then poked a single to left. White and Dent scored for the Yankees fourth and fifth runs of the inning. When the scoring finally ended, the Yanks had tallied seven runs and driven Eckersley to the showers.

Incredibly, the Yankees had won three straight at Fenway and demoralized the entire city of Boston. "I've had my heart broken by the Sox many times," said one fan, "but what happened in those three games just ripped my heart to shreds."

Fred Lynn tried to joke off the shock. "They must be cheating," he said. "Those aren't the same Yankees we saw before. I really think George Steinbrenner used his clone money. I think those were Yankee clones that were being used out there from those great Yankee teams of the past."

A Boston writer groaned, "It's the first time a team has been in first place by a game—and trailing."

The real mood of the Boston players was captured by Carlton Fisk. "How can a team get thirty-something games over .500 in July and then in September see its pitching, hitting and fielding all fall apart at the same time?"

Guidry's 7–0 whitewash was only the second complete game turned in by a left-hander against Boston in 1978, and he was the first southpaw to blank them at Fenway since 1974. "This team is loaded with tough guys," said Reggie Jackson, attempting to explain the Yankee turnaround. "This team is loaded with professionals."

Game four pitted rookie Bobby Sprowl of Boston

against Ed Figureroa. A couple of months earlier Sprowl had hurled for the Bristol Red Sox. Sprowl articulated Don Zimmer's instructions. "My only objective is to keep us in the game. I am not expecting to pitch a shutout." No one else expected him to, either.

For Boston fans and players, what happened in the first inning was like an old-time horror movie replayed. Sprowl walked Mickey Rivers. Sprowl walked Willy Randolph. Things looked hopeful for Boston when Munson grounded into a DP, but there was Reggie to contend with. Reggie singled in Rivers. Sprowl had lost his shutout. He walked Piniella. He walked Chambliss. Zimmer walked too. The harried Boston pilot replaced Sprowl with Bob Stanley, who gave up a two-run single to Nettles. The inning ended with the Yankees ahead, 3–0.

By the fourth inning, the Yanks led, 6–0. The final score of the game was Yankees 7, Sox 4. "HOLY COW," one newspaper headline declared, summarizing the entire frenetic turn of events, "IT'S TIED."

The statistics for the four games were completely lopsided. The Yanks pounded out 42 runs and notched 67 hits. Boston eked out just nine runs and managed just 21 hits. A dozen errors also contributed to the "Boston Massacre."

The record of the two teams from July 19 to September 10 was

Boston	24–28
New York	39–14

Carl Yastrzemski responded to all the flak by claiming, "It's never easy to win a pennant. We've got three weeks to play. Anything can happen. We've got three games in Yankee Stadium next weekend."

For Yaz, it was easier to look ahead than back at the four-game Yankee sweep—the first time since 1968 that the Sox had been swept in a four-game series at Fenway.

Jim Rice's 39th and 40th home runs of the season the next day gave the Red Sox a 5–4 win over Jim Palmer and Baltimore. It was the first errorless game played by Boston in 11 attempts. The win enabled the Sox to climb back into first place, a half-game ahead of the idle Yankees. "This win can turn us around," said Rice. "But we can't let up."

They did. After a loss to Baltimore and a double loss to the Indians, Boston, trailing the Yankees by 1½ games, came into Yankee Stadium on Friday, September 15, for a three-game series. The dissension and disharmony that had afflicted the Bronx Bombers like a bad summer cold had now seemingly been passed on to Boston.

Rick Burleson's griping typified the acrimony that afflicted the Sox. "The Yankees are together as a unit," he said, "and we are not. We don't know who's going to be in the lineup when we come to the park and that's a bunch of bleep. The way I see it the Yanks had a guy, Jackson, who comes out of the hospital to play in the series against us. That's how much it meant to them. We have a guy who pulls himself out of a game after making a couple of errors. [A reference to Dwight Evans, who removed himself from the third game at Fenway Park after he had made two miscues against the Yankees.] Just having Evans in there would have been helpful to the last two games."

Former Boston announcer Ken Harrelson remembers arriving at the stadium with the Sox: "It was kind of unbelievable coming off the bus and walking through the crowd out there, with so many of them screaming out four-letter words, and witnessing all that aggression against the Red Sox. There were a lot of sick people."

Amid extensive media coverage and extra security personnel, Yankee Stadium crackled with tension as Luis Tiant warmed up for the Sox and Ron Guidry readied himself for the Bronx Bombers. Thousands of BoSox rooters had made the trek to New York City to support their team. "The damn guy's not Superman," one of them yelled at a Yankee fan. "Guidry's going to lose today."

If he wasn't Superman, he was managing to perpetrate a good impersonation. Guidry allowed just two hits as he pitched a route-going 4–0 shutout. It was the 42nd win in 56 games for the Yanks. The "Big Push" was a steamroller. The Yanks had extended their lead over Boston to 2½ games.

Catfish Hunter opposed Mike Torrez in the second game of the series on Saturday. Jim Rice's 41st homer of the year gave the Sox a 2–0 lead in the first inning. A Reggie Jackson single brought the Yanks within a run of the Sox in the bottom of the first and then the outspoken outfielder homered in the fifth inning to tie the score. Jackson had batted .317 since Billy Martin's exit.

The game moved to the bottom of the ninth inning with the scored tied, 2–2. Torrez and Hunter had matched each other virtually pitch for pitch. With two strikes on him, Mickey Rivers smacked the ball over the head of Yastrzemski, who was playing a shallow left field and shading the foul line. Rivers turned on the speed and wound up on third base with a triple. "If it had been me," Rivers said later, "and it was that late in a game that meant so much, I would have played me a lot deeper than he did." Rivers was underscoring the acrimony between the two clubs. Munson collected another RBI as Rivers came across the plate to give the Yanks a 3–2 win.

Bob Lemon, grandfatherly, kindly, unassuming, emerged more and more as a Yankee folk hero. It was reported that he called up his wife after the 3–2 victory and told her how much fun he was having winning. "This is even better than sex!" he joked.

Yastrzemski was not in a joking mood. The soul and spirit of the Boston team, he had been the goat designated by the media for the way he played Rivers. Before the fatal pitch to the slight Yankee outfielder, Yaz had moved in about a half dozen steps and crowded the left-field foul line. "I didn't want Rivers on base. I thought he might bloop one in or hit a line drive that I would not be able to catch. I wanted to keep him off base. He could steal off Mike's big windup." And then, underscoring the confusion, the pulling in opposite directions that many noted about the Sox, Yaz added, "The pitch was supposed to be low and inside. It wound up over the plate where he could go with it to left."

With 14 games to play, the Yanks led by 3½ games. "We have to win them all," said Yastrzemski.

Burleson was not so optimistic. "The abuse we've taken and the abuse we must be prepared to take we richly deserve."

One Yankee player provided his perspective: "Boston is so tight that you couldn't get a needle up their asshole. They choke."

The Sox, behind Dennis Eckersley, revived in the third game of the series as they pounded three Yankee pitchers for eleven hits and a 7–3 win. Even George Scott contributed. With nothing to show for his last 36 at-bats, he cracked a double in the eighth inning. Instead of the Yankee lead being stretched to 4½ games, Boston had whittled it back to 2½.

With 13 games left to play, the Sox were being battered by the Boston press and second-guessed by some of their fans. Charges of the Sox choking, of flinching, of losing their nerve, were the main topics of conversation all over New England.

Incredibly, all the abuse seemed to stoke the Sox to greater effort. Instead of folding up their tents and sinking further down in the American League East, they caught fire. It wasn't that the Yankees faltered, it was just that the Sox went on a tear, as the following table reveals.

		BOSTON (Games Behind)
September 19	Boston 8, Detroit 6	
	Milwaukee 2, New York 0	1½
September 20	(doubleheader)	
	Toronto 8, New York 1	
	New York 3, Toronto 2	
	Detroit 12, Boston 2	2
September 21	New York 7, Toronto 1	
	Boston 5, Detroit 1	2
September 22	Cleveland 8, New York 7	
	Toronto 5, Boston 4	2
September 23	Boston 3, Toronto 1	
	Cleveland 10, New York 1	1

September 24	New York 4, Cleveland 0	
	Boston 7, Toronto 6	1
September 26	Boston 6, Detroit 0	
	New York 4, Toronto 1	1
September 27	Boston 5, Detroit 2	
	New York 5, Toronto 1	1
September 28	Boston 1, Detroit 0	
	New York 3, Toronto 1	1
September 29	Boston 11, Toronto 0	
	New York 3, Cleveland 1	1
September 30	New York 7, Cleveland 0	
	Boston 4, Toronto 1	1
October 1	Cleveland 9, New York 2	
	Boston 5, Toronto 0	———

The season came down to the final three games for both the Red Sox and Yankees. Only one game separated baseball's greatest rivals. No longer were the "choke" charges being tossed about at Boston. All of New England was in a frenzy. Every pitch of Yankee and Red Sox games was labored over by millions of fans. Like two punchy fighters, neither willing to quit, or knowing how to quit, the archrival Red Sox and Yankees played out the string. The Sox took two games from Toronto while the Yanks (with their eyes on the scoreboard) won two games from Cleveland to close out September.

On the first day of October, the last day of the regular season, the American League East standings revealed that the Yankees still clung to a one-game lead over Boston. A Boston loss or a Yankee win would clinch the division title for the Bronx Bombers. It wasn't fated to happen that way. The Yanks went down to a 9–2 defeat as the Indians pounded Catfish Hunter and his successors. At Fenway, the Sox racked up their eighth straight win, and their 12th victory in the last 15 games. Both teams finished the season with identical records of 99–63, setting the stage for the second one-game play-off in American League history.

All those years of coming in second behind the Yankees were evoked as the city of Boston and the Sox faithful girded for the 1978 play-off game. There were many in New England who through the years had been beset by bitter memories; they wondered if they would have one more nightmare to add to the collection that woke them up in the middle of the night with a vision of a Yankee crossing home plate with a winning, heartbreaking run against the Sox.

"Coming into Fenway," Phil Pepe recalls, "the Yankees were sky-high for that final game. They had wiped out Boston in those four games. They had momentum. They had Guidry pitching—they thought he was invincible . . . and there was Gossage to back him up. . . . The only thing that I guess was in everyone's mind amidst the tension and excitement was that it was a game in Fenway Park and anything could happen."

The scene was out of Hollywood casting: October 2, 1978, Yankees versus Red Sox at Fenway Park. Boston's 1978 home attendance was 2,320,643—just 15,000 behind that of the Yankees, who led the American League playing in a much bigger park. New York had triumphed in nine of the 16 games played between the two teams to take the season series, but the Sox had performed at a .720 clip at Fenway, winning 59 of its 82 games there.

Boston was the "hot team" and had the home field advantage, but the Yankees had Guidry (24–3) and, if nec-

The view from the bleachers at Fenway Park, jammed with fans for a Yankee–Red Sox encounter

essary, Gossage (26 saves). Much was made of the fact that Guidry was going to pitch with only three days' rest. "It's only one game," Guidry responded. "And one game is enough—I can pitch one game." Also out of Hollywood casting was Guidry's opponent, Torrez, who just the year before had worn Yankee pinstripes and was now pitted against his former teammates, determined to beat them.

Almost 33,000 crowded into Fenway to watch the action and millions more saw the game over national television or heard it on their local radio stations. "That one game surpasses any other one I've ever been connected with," recalls Yankee broadcaster Frank Messer. "Those two teams . . . and the whole season boiling down to just one game at Fenway. . . . It was quite a moment for everyone who was there or who watched it on TV."

In the second inning, Yastrzemski stoked a home run

21

down the right-field line to give Boston a 1–0 lead. "Guidry wasn't the same guy we saw earlier," said Fred Lynn.

"I thought that when the old man [Yaz] hit the home run that was going to do it. Mike [Torrez] was throwing the ball real well and he wanted that win," said former Boston announcer Hawk Harrelson.

In the third inning, Scott doubled off the center-field wall, giving Guidry another lump; the Sox did not score, but they were hitting the invincible man and gaining confidence with each turn at bat. They generated some more offense in the fourth and fifth inning. Then, in the sixth, Burleson cracked a double and Remy bunted him over to third base. Jim Rice singled. Burleson came home, making the score 2–0 Boston. Fred Lynn came up. He mashed Guidry's pitch deep to right field. "I lost the ball for a moment in the sun," recalls Piniella, "but I recovered and fortunately was able to make the catch." Guidry had been on the ropes but Boston couldn't batter him out.

As the Yankees came to bat in the seventh, there was a feeling of confidence among many Boston rooters. Torrez had yielded no runs and just two hits to this point. Then Chambliss singled. White singled. Lemon yanked Brian Doyle and sent Jim Spencer in as a pinch hitter. Spencer flied out. Sox fans relaxed a bit. The light-hitting Bucky Dent was the next scheduled batter.

A .140 hitter for the final 20 games of the season, Dent had managed to hit only four home runs during 1978. Dent choked up on the bat, just seeking to make contact. Torrez pitched and Bucky fouled the ball off his foot, stinging an old injury from earlier battles in that frenetic season. Dent moved about trying to shake off the sting.

The man they like to forget in Boston—Bucky Dent, Yankee shortstop

"Mickey Rivers was on deck," recalls Messer, "and he noticed a crack in Bucky's bat. He called it to Bucky's attention." Dent decided to switch bats and stepped back in to face Torrez with a Mickey Rivers bat.

In their dugout, the Yankees were screaming encouragement to Dent. In the stands, fans were exhorting Torrez to greater effort.

"Hit the tin, Bucky," screamed Reggie Jackson, beseeching Dent to pound the ball off the left-field wall and drive in the two runs on base.

The 6′5″ Torrez went into his windup and hurled his pitch to the 5′9″ Dent. Bucky got good wood on the ball. "The fact that it was at Fenway Park," recalls Messer, "as soon as it left the bat I thought it had a chance. Any time you hit a fly ball in Boston there's a chance."

The ball cleared the infield and climbed in the outfield toward the left-field wall—the Green Monster. Yaz, who had been in that position many times before, moved back, back, back on instinct, toward the wall. The ball went over the "tin." And as Bucky raced around first base he knew the shot had landed in the left-field net.

Roy White and Chris Chambliss waited at home plate to pound out their congratulations on Bucky as the Yankee dugout spilled out with awe and applause at what Dent had done. With the Yankees now leading in the game, 3–2, Fenway Park was silent. Stunned Boston fans could not believe what had taken place. An instant before the Sox and Torrez had been in complete control—and now the Yankees had taken charge.

So unnerved was Torrez by what had happened that he went to a full count on Rivers and walked him. That was all for Torrez. Bob Stanley came in to pitch. Rivers stole

Lou Piniella, who loves to play at Fenway in a Yankee uniform

second base. Munson punched a double to deep center and the Yankee lead was now 4–2.

In the bottom of the seventh inning, a George Scott single ended Guidry's stint on the mound. Gossage came in to pitch. He had a string of thirty appearances in which he had yielded no home runs while recording 15 saves and six wins. The Sox did not score in the seventh.

"That seventy-eight play-off game is something I'll never forget," says Lou Piniella. "I can still vividly remember standing out in right field in the latter part of that game wanting the game to get over. We had the lead on Bucky's home run. We had the Goose in there to short-circuit them. But we knew that Boston was at home and that Boston was going to come back at us. It was probably the most exciting game I ever played in."

In the Yankee eighth, Reggie Jackson tagged a Bob Stanley fastball deep into the center-field bleachers. The Yankees now led, 5–2. "When it wound up in the bleachers," says Jackson, "I just thought it was an extra run."

The game moved to the home half of the eighth inning. Fenway was a frenzy of Boston fans cheering on the Sox. Remy doubled off Gossage. Bedlam prevailed. Yaz singled him home. The little ballpark rocked with noise. Carlton Fisk singled. Lynn singled to score Yastrzemski and bring the Sox within a run of the Yankees. Gossage got Hobson on a fly ball. Scott was the batter. Thousands were on their feet cheering, beseeching the powerful batter to hit it out. Lemon remained calm while all around him there was bedlam. He stayed with Gossage, who reached back and struck out Scott with one of his fiery fastballs.

The Yankees went out swiftly in the top of the ninth

inning, and the entire season for the two archrivals came down to the Sox' last three outs in the bottom of the ninth.

With one out, Burleson managed to work a walk against Gossage. Remy, the contact hitter, stepped in. Gossage pitched carefully, perhaps too carefully. The Goose seemed to aim his pitch to the plate and Remy slashed the ball to right field. It kept sinking. The sun and the moment bore down on Piniella, who lost the ball for a moment, and it dropped in front of him. He trapped the ball at the last instant, and fired it to third base. Eddie Yost, screaming from the coach's box at third for Burleson to come on, watched in amazement as the runner hesitated and finally remained at second base. The Yankees were not out of it just yet.

Jim Rice, who had connected for 28 homers that season at Fenway, came to the plate bidding for number 29. He slammed a Gossage fastball to deep right field. His swing was a bit late and he didn't get all of the ball. Piniella did. Burleson tagged up and moved on to third base.

The Sox were down to their last out. It was fated to be a dramatic battle right down to this final sequence. Carl Yastrzemski was the batter. In his 18th season with the Sox, Yaz faced the Goose with a record of 17 homers, 81 RBIs, 76 walks against just 44 strikeouts and nine double plays hit into in the 1978 season. He accomplished all this despite back and wrist injuries that vexed and hobbled him all through the year. Durable, dependable, Yaz was the darling of the Red Sox fans. It was Boston's stylish slugger versus New York's power pitcher.

Burleson took his lead at third base. Remy took his lead at first base. Gossage took his signs from Munson.

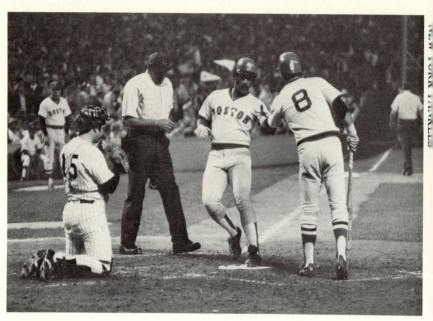

Yaz congratulates Jim Rice after the Sox outfielder hits a home run against the Yankees. Thurman Munson seems deep in thought

They were academic. "I wasn't going to mess around with breaking junk," the Goose would say later, "and get beaten by anything but my best. Yastrzemski's the greatest player I've ever played against. I just wound up and threw it as hard as I could. I couldn't tell you where."

Yaz took the first pitch for a ball. Burleson, the tieing run, grew edgy at third; Remy, the winning run, stretched his leg muscles at first. Jackson's homer, which had seemed superfluous at the time, was all that separated the two teams.

Gossage went into his windup. Around came the right arm—and a fastball tailing away from Yaz's power came to the plate. The Sox legend swung with full force, but all he could manage was to loft the ball in a gentle arc toward third base. Nettles gloved it near the coaching box at third. The Yankees won, 5–4.

For Boston, the end was bitter. Yaz marched back to his dugout, disgusted. The Yankees were whooping it up in their dugout. They had overcome a 14-game lead and beaten the Sox on their own turf in the most significant game of the season—the most crucial game of all the supercharged contests played by the two clubs over the years. Nettles jumped into the arms of Gossage as Yankee players poured out onto ancient Fenway's turf.

Jim Rice retreated to the trainer's room and refused to speak to the press after the game. He had pounded 46 homers and collected 139 RBI's, but the Sox had lost.

Yaz, disappointed but hopeful, said, "Someday, we're going to get that cigar. Before Old Yaz retires, he is gonna play on a world champion."

Fisk, angered and exhausted, said, "They caught us this time at our lowest ebb. We were hurting and our pitching was not consistent. When they came back they found out that we were the team with momentum. We had won eight in a row and to think that it came down after a 162-game schedule to one game. But we never quit—not once."

Steinbrenner, exultant with victory, was magnanimous. "Take nothing away from the Red Sox," he said. "They never quit."

For veteran Red Sox publicist Bill Crowley, who had been through many of the same situations, the words came with emotion: "We came in for that final game after losing the big lead with the fear hanging over us. We shouldn't even have been there. I remember all the national press that was literally sitting on the roof at Fenway and the Dent home run and the Yankee people delirious and the Boston people dazed. Many headed for a damn good drunk."

Filing out of Fenway, the Sox fans were both subdued and enraged. Like Don Zimmer, they had another nightmare to add to their collection—in Bill Crowley's phrase, "That damn ball that Dent hit going into the screen."

One middle-aged man had to finally be escorted out of Fenway Park about an hour after the game was concluded. "I love the rivalry," he told police, "but I hate the fucking Yankees."

THE MOOD

It is perhaps the oldest and strongest rivalry in American sports history—the Yankees of New York versus the Red Sox of Boston. It is a competition of teams, cities, styles, ballparks, fans and, at times, writers. Its roots reach back to Babe Ruth and Harry Frazee, but it is as contemporary as the next Red Sox–Yankee game.

Part of the rivalry is the stark contrast in the images of the two teams. The New York Yankees are one of the most successful of all franchises in baseball history. A club of legends: Ruth, Gehrig, Dickey, Ford, Berra, Munson, Raschi, Reynolds, Mantle, Maris, Jackson,

Guidry, Gossage. Through the years, winning has been as much a part of the Yankees' nature as the pinstriped uniforms, the monuments and plaques in deep center field. It was once said that "rooting for the Yankees is like rooting for General Motors." General Motors has fallen on tough times, but the Yankees roll on. They are the champions, the front runners, the *crème de la crème* of baseball.

The Red Sox, less successful, more human, more vulnerable, have seemed like the rest of us. For the team and their fans, winning at times has not seemed as important as beating the Yankees and then winning. For through the years, the success of the Sox has been measured against Yankee success.

Through the 1981 season, the Yankees are 896–715 against Boston, and there have been all the years of Sox runner-up finishes to the Bronx Bombers. In 1904, 1938, 1939, 1941, 1942, 1949, 1977 and 1978, the Yankees and Red Sox finished one–two in the American League standings. And each of those years except 1904, there was a Yankee pennant. For the fans of the old Brooklyn Dodgers, the slogan used to be, "Wait 'til next year." For Boston fans, it has been, "When are they going to fold this year?" The Sox have finished in second place 13 times, and more than half those finishes were behind the hated New York Yankees. The second-place blues have frustrated Sox rooters and further accentuated the Boston–New York rivalry.

The competition involves much more than a baseball team representing Boston against a baseball team representing New York. It is, in reality, a competition between the provincial capital of New England and the mega-municipality of New York City: the different life-styles of the people in those areas, the different accents they speak in, the contrasting symbols that are guideposts to their cities. It's the Charles River versus the East River; Boston Common compared with Central Park. History, culture, style, pace, dreams, self-images—all are mixed up in the competition in one way or another. And the fact that both teams have been in the American League since the beginning of the century doesn't hurt the rivalry either.

Bill Crowley, former Boston publicist, doesn't mince words: "Red Sox fans," he says, "hate the Yankees desperately. The pinstripes, the glamour, the hoopla—it is something that is very deeply resented. And when they win—especially over us—you can cast a pall over this whole area."

Red Sox' territory comprises 5½ states—Massachusetts, Vermont, Maine, Rhode Island, New Hampshire, and half of Connecticut.

"The Sox give away western Connecticut to the Mets and the Yankees," notes Crowley, "and there are pockets of resistance in Providence, Rhode Island, and Worcester, Massachusetts. Most of the pockets are Italian. The people there were fans of Yankee stars Crosetti, Lazerri, DiMaggio, Berra, Rizzuto—and they passed it on to their sons and grandsons."

Crowley had the unusual experience of being a Boston kid "who grew up to broadcast for the Yankees first." Crowley worked with Mel Allen broadcasting Yankee games. "That was thirty years ago. I was the third-string announcer, and Ralph Houk was the third-string catcher." It was back then that Crowley was made acutely aware of the Sox-Yankee Connecticut dividing line.

"Mel [Allen] was supersensitive," remembers Crowley,

who still smiles at the way things were in the early 50s and the way he worried that his wife, who was very pro-Red Sox, might say something at a dinner party or gathering and be overheard by Yankee general manager George Weiss, who was, of course, passionately anti-Red Sox. "We'd sit there at the Stadium for a Sunday double-header with the Sox. Fifty, sixty thousand people would show up and some of them would carry placards: 'EAST WATERBURY SAYS MEL ALLEN STINKS.' "

"Mel would get very upset," continues Crowley. "I'd say, 'Wait just a few minutes, Mel. West Waterbury will come by and everything will be all right.' A little while later West Waterbury did come by and their placards bragged: 'WEST WATERBURY THINKS MEL ALLEN IS GREAT.' "

Through the years, Yankee fans have been sated with the greatness and the spectacular dominance of the Bronx Bombers over their baseball competition. The Yanks have piled up 33 American League pennants and 22 world championships. Boston has managed just nine pennants and five world championships, the last one in 1918.

These statistics have contributed in part to Boston's bittersweet romance with its fans and its writers. Dubbed the "Olde Towne Teame," romanticized by authors John Updike and John Cheever, the Sox have been likened to a "bad broad." Summer romance usually turns into a jilting in the fall, but by spring the fans fall in love again, seemingly more deeply than ever.

The frustration with the "bad broad" and the losses to the New York Yankees has elicited some sharp rebukes from Boston writers. On June 1, 1950, one of them wrote,

"Look at them all out there—nice fellows, all well paid, all good players, but Birdie Tebbets excepted, there isn't enough spirit in the whole lot of them to provide enough flickering flame for one cigarette lighter."

An even more vituperative comment was made by Mike Barnicle in the September 9, 1979, *Boston Globe*. "What has 18 legs and no arm?" he wrote. "What folds easier than toilet paper? What baseball team can impersonate the main course of a Thanksgiving dinner? The Sox could qualify for a group rate on a heart transplant . . . they have looked like accordions or folding chairs. . . . They're an embarrassment, a very collection of dressing room fighters. They are a pathetic team without character."

Writers such as these have earned the reputation and the appellation of the vicious Boston press. "They are never satisfied," explains Bill Crowley. "They are like a combination of fan writers. They go to the winter baseball meetings and are impressed by a couple of trades and things they hear about the team. They go to spring training and again are impressed. 'This is going to be it.' And if it doesn't happen—like the disappointed bridegroom, they become extremely negative."

In 1946, 1967 and 1975 there was no negativism, no disappointed bridegroom. The atmosphere throughout New England in those years was unrestrained euphoria.

When the 1946 season began, some experts joked that "the Red Sox will win in their league and the Yankees will win in the American League." Seventh-place finishers in 1945, Boston had last won a pennant in 1918. The Yankees had reeled in six pennants in the nine years prior to the 1946 season.

Three all-time Sox stars: Bobby Doerr, Johnny Pesky and Ted Williams

On Opening Day of the 1946 season, it looked like the same old story. The Bronx Bombers pounded Tex Hughson and crushed Boston, 12–5. The next day, however, the Sox swamped the Yankees by the same score and were off on a 15-game winning streak. In May, Boston won 21 of 27 games.

By the All-Star break, the Red Sox were 54–23. It was a team led by farm products and fashioned to the contours of Fenway Park: Ted Williams, Bobby Doerr, Dom DiMaggio, Mickey Harris, Earl Johnson. More than 600,000 fans turned out to see the season series between the Red Sox and Yankees. Thousands more were turned away.

Posting a 60–17 record at home, the Sox won 104 games, the most in their history. They finished the season in first place with a .675 percentage, highest in their history. Boston also recorded its first million-attendance for a season, as 1,416,944 crowded into tiny Fenway to cheer on the home team.

Bitter Yankee fans blamed their team's disappointing third-place finish (17 games out) on slumps by Joe DiMaggio, Charlie Keller, Joe Gordon and Tommy Henrich. Jubilant Sox rooters simply bragged that Boston was the better team. Indeed, the Sox did win 15 of 22 games they played against the Yankees.

The '46 Sox were an exciting and talented club. Ted Williams batted .342 and recorded 38 home runs and 123 RBIs. He led the league in walks, runs scored, slugging percentage and total bases. Dom DiMaggio batted .316 and was a master center fielder. Pesky steadied the infield, batted .335, led the league in hits and was second in runs scored. Rudy York, acquired in a key trade, drove in 119 runs. The four starters solidified the team. "Boo"

Ferriss was 25–6; Tex Hughson was 20–11; Mickey Harris was 17–9; Joe Dobson was 13–7. And their task was made much simpler because of the potent Boston lineup that led the league in batting average, slugging percentage and runs scored.

If rooting for the Red Sox in 1946 was like eating a bowl of cherries, in the words of one sad Boston fan, "For long years after that, it was the pits."

The 1948 Sox defeated the New York Yankees twice in the last two days of the season, doing what they had to do. The first victory knocked the Yankees out of the pennant. The second victory set up the first single-game play-off in American League history. Some Boston zealots were more thrilled by the first win than the second. Cleveland defeated Boston in the play-off and the Sox finished in second place, a game off the pace.

In 1949, Boston came into Yankee Stadium with a one-game lead, needing a split in their two-game series to clinch the pennant. The Sox succumbed to the Yanks, 4–0, in the first game. And the Bronx Bombers, with a four-run eighth inning, won the second game, 5–3. It was the second straight second-place finish for the men from Fenway. Long years of mediocrity set in after that.

From 1949 to 1965, the Red Sox finished behind the Yankees in the standings. From 1960 to 1966, Boston was twice last, twice eighth, twice seventh, once sixth. Only in 1966 did the Sox finish ahead of the Yanks—in ninth place, a half-game ahead of the tenth-place New Yorkers.

Dick Williams took over as manager of the 1967 Red Sox. A rookie pilot, he had his work cut out for him. "There had been tremendous teams at Boston," Williams recalled, "but they had won just one pennant in twenty-

Boston Red Sox fan frenzy in the Miracle Year of 1967

one years. At home they were excellent, but they could just not win on the road because it was a team manufactured to play at Fenway Park."

Williams made up his mind not to allow the dimensions of Fenway to influence his managing and the play of his athletes. "I made it clear," Williams explained, "that the wall was not going to be a factor. I had seen too many players ruining themselves taking shots at the wall. I made my pitchers concentrate on pitching in to right-handed batters, who always came up there looking for the ball away thinking we'd try to get them to avoid pulling. I knew that the way to pitch at Fenway is to get the ball inside and gradually back the batter up a little."

They are still debating whether Williams's theory had anything to do with what happened or not—but Williams worked a miracle. The Sox, a 100–1 shot to win the pennant, proved the oddsmakers wrong. Behind the pitching of Jim Lonborg, who won 22 games, and the Triple Crown batting of Carl Yastrzemski (.326, 44 homers, 121 RBIs), the Sox climbed from ninth place to first place in one season. They were dubbed the "Cinderella Sox." Their accomplishment was called the "Impossible Dream." And Elston Howard, who came over from the hated enemy New York Yankees in midseason to help, exclaimed, "I never saw anything like this. And we won a lot of pennants when I was with New York."

There was another pennant for the Sox in 1975. And there was more rejoicing, for not only did Boston finish two notches higher than the Yankees, the Hub team outdrew New York in home attendance that season.

However, despite the banner seasons of 1946, 1967 and 1975, historically the cycle of Boston's Red Sox has always seemed to possess a recurring theme.

Just as Labor Day approaches and the Boston children prepare for school, and the zinnias and the marigolds in the Public Gardens bloom, the Sox have seemed to lag in their competitive quest. Through these Indian summers, fans keep coming to Fenway Park. Some fans come to boo. Others come to cry. And still others come to hope and pray.

Historically, the fans of the Red Sox rank among the

most loyal as well as the most excitable in all of baseball. The Sox, for example, drew more people into their little ballpark in the decade of the '70s than any other American League team. And when the competition is Yankee–Red Sox, it's one of the toughest tickets in all of sports, especially if both teams are in pennant contention. The Yankees through 1981 had drawn over one million on the road for 36 straight seasons, and in 1981 drew over a million to Yankee Stadium for the 44th time in their 79-year history. A good portion of those who came out came out to see them battle the Red Sox. In 1981 the Sox drew over a million fans into Fenway Park, the 15th straight year they topped that mark. Even more impressive is the fact that six times since 1967 Boston, with the smallest ballpark seating capacity in baseball, led the American League in attendance.

Boston attendance figures have ballooned through Yankee–Sox encounters. On given days, up to 10,000 fans have taken Eastern Airlines flights between Boston and New York. Some have made the flight to witness a single game; others have stayed for an entire series. There have been times when the television networks have been outdrawn in the ratings by local stations broadcasting the games between the two historic rivals. At diners, gas stations, roadside rests, zealots have congregated, contesting and censoring each other's opinions as they stop off on the long drives from Connecticut, Vermont, New Hampshire, Rhode Island, western Massachusetts, New Jersey, New York, North Carolina, Georgia . . . to Fenway or the Stadium.

Behind the scenes, Bob Fishel, first as a Yankee publicist and now performing some of the same duties with the

American League office, has seen the rivalry up close. "When I was with the Yankees," says Fishel, "we never had to promote the competition between the two teams. It didn't need promotions. It still doesn't. Even today people buy tickets months in advance for Yankee–Red Sox games. From a scheduling point of view in the American League office, a conscious attempt is made to schedule weekend games [and] late-season matchups to capitalize on the rivalry."

Fenway Park and Yankee Stadium, symbols of the two teams, are more than just home fields. Their sizes, shapes, locations and histories have influenced the rivalry and the makeup of the Red Sox and Yankee teams.

Boston first began play at Fenway Park in 1912, on the property of the Fenway Realty Company. Red-brick and human-scaled, still in the middle of town, still possessed of natural turf, still without the shopping-center parking lots, F.P. was once described as the "Old North Church of Professional Sport." The park occupies an entire city block. Van Ness Street runs behind first base. Jersey Street, behind third base, is a tree-lined city street that evokes turn-of-the-century memories. Right field borders on Ipswich, and Lansdowne Street runs behind left field. The bleachers seat 7,418; there are 12,274 grandstand seats, 13,250 boxes and 594 roof boxes. The total seating capacity of 33,536 makes the Back Bay ballyard the smallest park in major league baseball.

Single-decked and intimate, the facility has always been a nightmare environment for left-handed pitchers. Originally, the giant "Green Monster" wall defining the left-field area was only 300 feet, six inches from home plate down the line. Later, home plate was moved back,

Opening Day at Fenway Park in 1957. Red Sox manager Pinky Higgins and Yankee manager Casey Stengel await the throwing out of the first ball

and today the wall in left field is a mere 315 feet away from the power swing of a right-handed slugger. From bottom to top the wall scales 37 feet. Atop the wall is a screen that extends 23 feet. The barrier was placed there to cut down on the breakage of store windows on Landsdowne Street. Fans hang around after a game at Fenway to watch as an attendant catwalks along the top of the "Green Monster," collecting balls that were hit into the net during a game. Right field measures a mere 302 feet down the line, and 380 feet at its deepest, straightaway part. The previous distance was 400 feet straightaway, but bullpens erected to accommodate the left-handed power of

Ted Williams took away 20 feet. The bullpen walls are five feet high. The irregular contours of center field range from 420 feet at its deepest part to 390 at its shallowest portion. A little corner that abuts the center-field bleachers and the grandstand in right field is just another of the idiosyncracies that makes for interesting ball games and challenges for outfielders.

Once Fenway Park was a conglomeration of all types of advertising signs and posters. In 1934, when the park was completely refurbished, all of these commercial messages were removed. The only one left intact was a small board above the right-field roof corner that publicizes the Jimmy Fund, the house charity of the Red Sox. A few more signs have been added over the years, but in general the park is as it has always been. The brick grandstand on Jersey Street harkens back to the early days. Above the ticket window leading to the box seats above home plate there is a keystone that proclaims, "Fenway Park 1912."

Fenway's national bird is the pigeon. Fat from popcorn and Crackerjacks, these city birds squeeze into cracks and crevices and soar in flight in flocks at the crack of the bat or the roar of the crowd. And over the years the pigeons have even figured in the action on the field. In 1974, Willie Horton mortally wounded one of them with a foul ball. Another time a Fenway Park pigeon got in the way of a Hal Peck throw. In 1945, Skeeter Newsome doubled off a pigeon against the A's. The pigeon only lost a few tail feathers. The A's lost the game.

Pigeons, however, rarely influence the outcome of a game. The park does. "When we brought a Yankee ball club here," current Red Sox manager Ralph Houk notes, "that Green Monster fence always haunted me. It's always an exciting game here because of that fence. You never have a game won. You can have a four- or five-run lead going into the ninth and still lose a game.

"The park influences managing. You can't play for one run too early and you have to be careful with your pitching staff, especially if you're on a long home stand. You can mess up your bullpen and overwork your pitchers."

Phil Pepe, who has been in every major league park, singled out Fenway as "the greatest ballpark in America," adding, "it's one of the few parks that is a throwback to the old days." The *Daily News* sportswriter underscored how both Fenway and Yankee Stadium have shaped the look and the character of the Sox and Yanks over the years. "The Sox build their teams around right-handed power. They play for the big inning and not for one run. Left-handed pitchers traditionally in that park have not been the strong suit for the Sox. Conversely, the Yankees have been predominantly a left-handed hitting team because of the contours of the Stadium. When the Sox or Yankees find themselves in the other team's park, they find a lot of their power blunted. I remember a game at the Stadium where Fisk, Watson, Rice all hit shots—about six among them. The Yankee outfielders just camped under the balls and caught them for easy outs. Those three Sox players went back to the bench shaking their heads." In 1977, a season in which the Red Sox won just twice in eight attempts at Yankee Stadium, more than just "head shaking" accompanied the frustration. Game after game, deep blasts by Jim Rice, Butch Hobson, George Scott and Carlton Fisk went for long outs in the wide and deep spaces of left and center fields.

"Yankee Stadium was made for rabbits and giants," snarled Fisk. "You have to be a rabbit to catch a ball out there in the outfield and you have to be a giant to hit the ball out."

Joe DiMaggio had some of the same complaints that Fisk has about Yankee Stadium. "In the late forties," recalled the Yankee Clipper, "I hit a ball about four hundred feet to left center. We were playing the Red Sox, and my brother Dom had no trouble making the catch. Joe Gordon followed and hit one about 420 feet to the same area. Dom caught it. Then Yogi Berra cracked a line drive into the right-field seats near the foul line. If you remember, there was a low railing out there about three feet high. The ball barely cleared it. Yogi couldn't have hit that ball more than 300 feet. Joe Gordon and I watched him trot around the bases with a grin on his face. We looked at each other and shrugged our shoulders. If we were born left-handed, our shots would've landed in the bleachers. They didn't name that area in left-center field Death Valley for nothing."

So while the special dimensions of Yankee Stadium pose problems for teams, such as the Red Sox, built around right-handed power, the same obstacles exist for Yankee right-handed batters.

"I cry for days," says batting coach Charlie Lau, "when a right-handed batter hits a ball four hundred and thirty feet and it is an out. I think when you hit a ball that far, you should be rewarded for it. However, that's the way the park is. And Yankee left-handed hitters often have trouble in Fenway, so it evens out."

The pitching profile of the Sox and Yanks also provides an interesting contrast. "The Yankees are a pre-

The House That Ruth Built—packed with fans

dominantly left-handed team," notes Pepe, "because left-handed pitching has an advantage at Yankee Stadium. But when the Yankees go to Fenway Park, just as their left-handed hitting power advantage is taken away, the left-handed pitching advantage that exists at the Stadium is also muted at Fenway ... although Guidry, May and John and others have won there in recent years."

Mickey Mantle, who starred for all those years in both parks, has special memories of both. "I loved to play at Fenway Park," he says. "But center field there was kinda tough. There were all those angles and the short center field fence. Down here at the Stadium you could run for two days in the outfield. There you had to watch it. You'd turn around and smash into the fence."

The final game at the old Yankee Stadium was played on September 30, 1973. There were 32,238 in attendance, including the widows of Babe Ruth and Lou Gehrig. The new Yankee Stadium is lots of white paint and blue seats. The drab gray look has been replaced by a dressed-up, regal, almost royal image that makes the park contrast even more dramatically to the small, green-toned Fenway.

Refurbished and remodeled, the playing field at the Stadium covers approximately 3.5 acres of the 11.6 total stadium acreage. A combination of nearly 800 incandescent and multivapor lamps lights up the field, projecting powers up to 1500 watts. The new scoreboard, electronic and massive, cost thirty times what Colonel Jake Ruppert paid to purchase Babe Ruth from the Red Sox. And the scoreboard's girth and size has eliminated the special views many once had from the 161st Street station of the IRT subway and the rooftops of adjacent apartment houses.

At every game at the Stadium, almost as a taunt to cities such as Boston, the huge electronic sound system pipes out the voice of Frank Sinatra singing, "If I can make it here, I'll make it anywhere / It's up to you, New York, New York." Another phrase in the song refers to those "little town blues," underscoring the differences between the Red Sox and the Yankees and the parks they play in.

Although Boston is by no means a "little town," it's not New York. "When the Yankees sell out on any given date today," explains Bill Crowley, "their gross income is about $700,000; their park seats 57,545, or 24,009 more than Boston. When the Sox sell out they don't even approach $400,000. With that gap in income, it's imperative that Boston have large numbers of fans coming to the ballpark to stay competitive. And even so, the Sox are not able to jump freely into the free-agent market and get the Winfields, Hunters, Johns, Jacksons."

If the contrasting sizes of the cities and the parks of the Yankees and Sox help shape the rivalry, the "mix" of fans is another element that affects the mood.

"The crowd at Yankee Stadium is definitely pro-Yankee," notes Frank Messer, "and pro-Boston at Fenway. However, the crowds are never that one-sided, because of the 'geography.' "

The "geography" involves many New Yorkers attending college in the Boston area who come to Fenway and sit in the bleachers, sometimes outnumbering Sox fans. These exiles come to root the Yankees on. The "geography" is also an intermingling of New Englanders at the Stadium, some cheering on the Sox, others rooting for the Yankees. In New York City there is even a faction of former Brooklyn Dodger and New York Giant fans who have attached themselves to the Sox; they come to the Stadium and demonstrate a fanatical devotion to Boston.

"I am especially aware of the mix at Fenway Park," says Lou Piniella. "There's a lot of excitement in that small park that makes it special. You might have twenty thousand Red Sox fans at Fenway and fifteen thousand Yankee fans. Their rivalry helps our rivalry. It excites the players, who have to respond to it."

Red Sox outfielder Dwight Evans is not as enamored with the atmosphere at Yankee Stadium as Piniella is

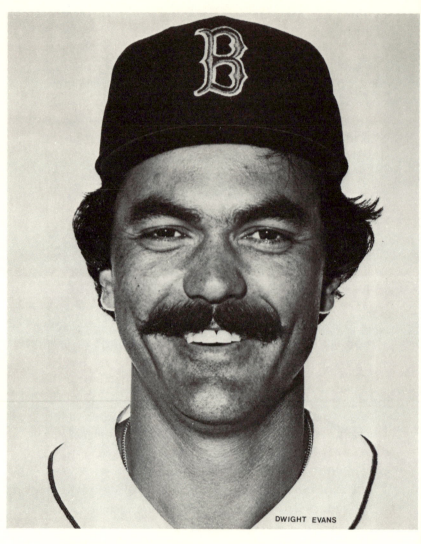

Dwight "Dewey" Evans—one of today's Sox stars

with that of Fenway Park. Evans made his first appearance at the Stadium in 1972 and has been there many times since in his Boston uniform. "When you have a Coke bottle go by your head from the third deck and they miss you by six inches, you wonder what kind of people these are. When you have cherry bombs thrown at you or thrown into crowds, that's not fun and that's not fans. Don't get me wrong—but I think the people that are crazy in New York are more crazy than the ones in Boston, and you've got crazy people there, too. When they say this is the Bronx Zoo, I agree. I think the majority of people that come to the Stadium are great, knowledgeable baseball fans, but they know what I mean when I talk about the crazy people that are there. I've had to wear helmets out there in the outfield many times. It's a great ballpark to play in, yet you have to watch out for things. When they throw a penny or a dime from the third deck and it hits you, it's going to put a knot on your head. They used to throw glass balls at me, broken glass wrapped in masking tape. And when it hit you, it punctured. Think about trying to play in the outfield and having things thrown at you all game long. I like people who like baseball, but not the nuts."

On the field, inside the white lines, the rivalry has been characterized by some of baseball's wildest moments.

In the first game ever played at Fenway Park, on April 12, 1912, the Sox trimmed the Yankees, 7–6, in 11 innings. The game was finally played after it had been rained out for three successive days.

On August 12, 1934, what was then the largest crowd in Fenway Park history assembled to see the two archrivals go at each other. They split a doubleheader, and Babe

Ruth, whose career was spent largely with the two teams, played his last game in a Yankee uniform at Fenway.

Another single-day game attendance record was set on August 7, 1956, as 36,350 watched as the Sox defeated the Yankees, 1–0, in 11 innings. Ted Williams walked with the bases loaded to drive in the winning run. "Terrible Ted" was so infuriated at not being given a chance to swing his bat that he sprayed Fenway Park with saliva. Tom Yawkey fined him $5,000. To this day Williams maintains that he never paid the fine.

Awesome and unpredictable rallies have contributed to the wild mood in the meetings between the Yankees and Red Sox. The Yanks had a seven-run ninth inning in 1940, an 11-run seventh inning in 1952, a 13-run fifth inning in 1945, a ten-run fourth inning in 1915, a six-run eleventh in 1970, an eight-run ninth in 1937. In 1954, the Sox had a 5–1 lead in the first game of a doubleheader and lost. They were trailing 7–0 in the second game and won; Jimmy Piersall's homer off Johnny Sain was the big blow for Boston. There are still those who remember Mel Parnell and the Sox leading New York 9–0 on Opening Day at Fenway and the nine-run eighth inning that gave the Yanks a 15–10 victory. In 1981, Boston pulled out an 8–5 win with a seven-run eighth-inning rally. On August 29, 1967, both clubs struggled through 19 innings until the Yankees prevailed in the 20th with a 4–3 win.

Many still talk about the long summer of 1949, when the Yanks and Sox raced for the pennant playing out their drama in jammed stadiums before rabid fans. The tension and the excitement seemed to be recharged each day.

The Mood

Those who witnessed and those who were the principal characters still talk about the day Cliff Mapes threw Johnny Pesky out at home plate on the Fourth of July at Yankee Stadium. Pesky was the runner at third. Al Zarilla hit the ball to right field. "All of a sudden," Rizzuto recalls, "this big cloud of something covered the sun. Holy Cow! Cliff Mapes loses the ball in the sky. It drops in." Pesky, bewildered, confused, finally broke for home. "And the throw by Mapes," smiles Rizzuto, "beat him."

With only two weeks to go in the 1949 campaign, fate once again positioned Pesky at third base. The Yankees and the Red Sox were tied in the standings and were clawing and scratching at each other, trying to pull out a victory. Darkness was descending rapidly. Bobby Doerr dropped down a surprise bunt to squeeze Pesky home. Tommy Henrich, corseted to cushion back-injury pains and playing first base, picked up the bunt. His throw to the Yankee catcher Ralph Houk appeared to have beaten the scrappy Sox infielder, but plate umpire Bill Grieve ruled that Pesky was safe.

Pandemonium prevailed. The Yankees protested long and loud. It was useless. Stengel drew a $150 fine. Houk and Mapes were fined $200 each. The Sox won the game, 5–4. And Pesky to this day insists, "I was safe. Ralph left a bit of the plate unblocked. I slid into that little bit of the plate under his tag."

It's more than 30 years since that slide. Pesky is a Red Sox coach and Houk, his former Yankee adversary, is now the manager of the Red Sox. Pesky provides an invaluable perspective on the rivalry, the changing nature of fans, the relationships among players:

Allie Reynolds was a peach of a guy. Lopat, Raschi—they were decent people. If they pitched you close, you didn't bother to look out there because they'd say, "If you didn't like that one—how about this one?" And the next one would be even closer. They didn't want to hurt you. They always thought that if they couldn't get you out with their ability as pitchers they didn't belong out there. Truthfully, I think there was affection. There was tough, hard competition, but there was respect. If you didn't love Yogi Berra or Phil Rizzuto, there was something wrong with you. And playing back then, there was real awe of the guys who would be double super-stars today, DiMag, Williams—people like that. The rivalry has been great for the teams and the cities, but it has gotten a lot of people in Boston upset, especially when it's gotten out of hand. When I go into Yankee Stadium today, I see so many people getting into jams in the stands there. That was unheard of when I played. The profanity, the physical violence—they'll wear the "Red Sox Sucks" tee shirts today, and then they'll come over and ask you for an autograph.

Pesky's point of view notwithstanding, the record clearly shows that the rivalry has intermittently flared into rage, and occasionally into violence. Sometimes it has been triggered by personality clashes; other times it has surfaced out of the frenzy with which the two teams historically have gone at each other.

In 1938, players from both clubs stormed the mound at the Stadium when Jake Powell of the Yankees and Boston's Joe Cronin started punching at each other. The flashpoint for the battle royal was Powell's rushing out to the mound to throttle Sox southpaw Archie McKain. Cronin was ejected from the game. Moments later, he was assaulted by several Yankee players under the stands.

The following year the Sox and Yanks engaged in a stalling contest. Lots of nasty language accentuated the slow-motion tactics. The game was forfeited in favor of the Yankees by umpire Cal Hubbard, who later was overruled by American League president Will Harridge. A storm of debris dumped by irate Yankee fans greeted Boston players when they visited the Stadium.

In 1947, a year in which the Yankees reeled off 19 straight victories, New York's Joe Page pitched fast and close to many Sox batters during a night game at Fenway. Bobby Doerr received an especially thorough dusting. Later in the game, Doerr had apparently stolen third base but was called out. Echoing their 1939 Yankee counterparts, Boston fans showered Fenway and New York players with garbage.

In 1952, Fenway Park was the scene of one of the most famous of Sox-Yankee physical altercations. Jimmy Piersall was a Boston rookie. "Hey Pinocchio," he screamed at Billy Martin. "Too damn yellow to fight me?" Piersall's commentary was a not-too-subtle reference to the contours of Martin's nose.

"Put up," snarled Martin, "or shut up your dumb ass. Let's settle this under the stands right now!"

Martin entered the Yankee dugout, Piersall went into the Sox dugout, and they circled under the stands for the violent rendezvous. Yankee coach Bill Dickey trailed after Martin and pitcher Ellis Kinder of Boston ran after Piersall.

Piersall and Martin faced each other. There were some more unprintable words, and then Martin jabbed two powerful shots to Piersall's face. Bleeding profusely from the nose, Piersall dropped to the ground. Dickey and Kinder moved between Piersall and the raging Martin, ending the one-sided battle.

In the Yankee dugout, Casey Stengel learned about what had happened. "That was all right," said Casey, who regarded Martin as a son. "I'm happy as long as he fights with the other teams and doesn't start with any players on the Yankees."

Perhaps the most famous on-the-field physical confrontation in the history of Sox-Yankee encounters took place on August 1, 1973. Both teams were battling for the lead in the American League East. Two nights before, the Yanks had scored twice in the ninth inning in the opener of the series to tie the game. The Sox scored once in the home half of the ninth to win. The Yankees had scored three times in the ninth inning of the second game of the series to win their first Fenway Park victory in a year.

What happened that August 1, 1973, epitomized the frenzy of the rivalry and underscored the raging debate over the relative abilities of Boston catcher Carlton Fisk and Yankee backstop Thurman Munson. The bickering evoked memories of New York City baseball's contentious conflict among fans that focused on who was the best center fielder: Willy Mays of the Giants, Duke Snider of the Dodgers or Mickey Mantle of the Yankees. The argument was never resolved, but a residue of negative feelings was part of the process. Fisk that summer had led in the All-Star balloting for catcher. Munson was voted runnerup. "That was part of the conflict," explains Frank Messer, "and there was even some personality conflict between the two of them."

The August 1 game was tied, 2–2, as the ninth inning

began. Sparky Lyle was the Yankee pitcher. John Curtis was on the mound for the Sox. Munson opened the New York ninth with a double down the left-field line and moved to third base on an infield ground out by Nettles. Gene Michael missed a squeeze bunt, but Munson came tearing down the line attempting to score. He slammed into Fisk, who was holding the ball and blocking the plate. The two catchers collided, but Fisk held on to the ball. Munson was out. Fisk shoved the Yankee catcher off his body, and Munson punched him in the face, bruising his left eye. Then the two catchers went into a clinch. Michael, Munson's roommate, got in a few punches of his own at Fisk. And then 61-year-old Fenway Park swarmed with players pushing, shoving, cursing. The playing field erupted with anger. More than 60 players and coaches, even those from the bullpens 350 feet away, got into the action, to the delight of many of the 30,689 fans.

When order was restored, Munson and Fisk were ejected from the game. "There's no question," Munson said later. "I threw the first punch, but he started it and then my roomie got into it. Fisk was lucky he didn't get into a fight last night the way he blocked the plate on Roy White."

"Munson and I were just bumping chests," Fisk later explained. "I flipped him off, but the big thing started when Michael got into it."

Michael was allowed to remain in the game, and this triggered another long delay as the Sox protested loudly and the partisan fans screamed out their rage.

When the Sox finally came to bat in the bottom of the ninth inning, Mario Guerrero singled in Bob Montgomery, who had replaced Fisk, to give Boston a 3–2 victory and drop the Yankees out of first place. Ironically, Guerrero was the player-named-later in the Sparky Lyle–Danny Cater trade. Even more ironically, Lyle lost for the fifth straight time, and his second time in three games, to his former Boston teammates, players he had openly antagonized as a result of the many negative comments he had made about them after the trade.

The crossover of Sparky Lyle on March 22, 1972, from the Red Sox to the Yankees was unusual. Perhaps the memory of Babe Ruth moving from the Sox to New York and becoming one of the greatest stars in baseball history put somewhat of a damper on trades between the rivals. Whatever the case, transactions between the Yankees and Sox have been minimal since Ruth's time.

Lyle's movement from the Sox to the Yankees was one of the worst deals Boston ever made. "When I was with Boston," recalls Lyle, "the Red Sox players and fans treated me well. I was made to feel part of the team and there was never any animosity. But after the trade, sometimes people came up to me at banquets and said, 'I can't root for you anymore because you're with the damn Yankees now.' I thought that was good. At least they were rooting."

Ironically, the trade for Lyle was engineered by Ralph Houk, then the Yankee manager and general manager. Houk, known as the Major, went from the Yankees to Detroit to retirement, and then was named skipper of the Red Sox on October 27, 1980.

At the winter baseball meetings in 1980, notes Bill Crowley, "Houk was asked to recall what was the best trade he was ever involved in."

" 'Sparky Lyle,' was Ralph's answer.

" 'Hey, Ralph,' I said. 'You're on our side now.'

" 'So what, Bill? It was still the best trade I ever made.' "

The Major, who battled the Red Sox for many years while in a Yankee uniform, admits it was a bit strange at first to be wearing a Boston Red Sox uniform. "But it was not as bad as when I first left the Yankees and went to Detroit. The fact that I didn't come directly from New York to Boston softened things. When you are away from an organization for a while, many of the players are not the same any more. It made it easier for me not competing against that many players I had known personally."

Joe McCarthy, one of the more famous crossovers, didn't have the same feelings as Houk. He was deeply involved with both teams. Yankee manager from 1931 to 1946, he piloted the Bronx Bombers to seven pennants, including four in a row (1936–1939). He won titles with such regularity that he was dubbed the Push Button Manager. In 1948, McCarthy took over as Red Sox manager. Appearing at a winter banquet, he was introduced to Johnny Pesky. "I remember your first home run in 1942, Pesky," snapped McCarthy. "It beat my Yankees."

"It's all right, Joe," smiled Pesky. "I'll be more than happy to return the favor."

One of the questions that was always asked of McCarthy was his opinion as to who was the greatest player, Joe DiMaggio or Ted Williams. "When I was with the Yankees," Marse Joe answered with diplomacy, "I was crazy about DiMag. Now that I'm with the Red Sox, I'm crazy about Williams."

The most famous rumored deal between the Red Sox

and Yankees involved Ted Williams and Joe DiMaggio. As the story goes, one night in 1947, Sox owner Tom Yawkey and Yankee boss Dan Topping were talking and drinking, drinking and talking at Toots Shor's. The banter focused on just how much better Williams would hit at Yankee Stadium and Joe DiMaggio would perform at the Fens. The banter allegedly concluded in the wee small hours of the morning with a handshake between the two men and an agreement on a trade of DiMaggio for Williams.

It was reported that when Topping arrived home and realized what he had agreed to, he picked up the phone and called Yawkey at 4:00 A.M. Topping's tone was one of panic. "Tom, I'm sorry, but I can't go through with the deal."

"Thank God," Yawkey allegedly replied.

Another version of the DiMaggio-Williams trade has Yawkey placing the phone call: "Dan, I know it's almost 5:00 A.M., and it's late, and I still want to make that trade we discussed. However, if you want to make it you'll have to throw in that little left-handed hitting outfielder, the odd-looking rookie."

"I can't." Topping was panicked. "We have big plans for him. We want to make him into a catcher. I'm afraid we'll have to call off the deal."

As everyone knows, DiMaggio and Williams played out their careers with the Yankees and Red Sox, and the little left-handed hitting outfielder remained a Yankee and became a catcher. His name was Yogi Berra.

Although the rivalry has had relatively few trades in recent years, it has probably spawned more hate mail, obscene letters and assassination threats than any other rivalry in baseball.

In August 1953 a letter arrived at Yankee Stadium, addressed to Mickey Mantle:

Hello . . . Mickey

Tom Umphlette got you 50 to 1. Don't show your face in Boston again or you're [*sic*] baseball career will come to an end with a 32. . . .

Remember I make almost every RED SOX and cheater Yankees game and I'll be sure to be there September 7. I've got a good gang that don't [*sic*] like the Yankees and you'll find out if you play the series starting September 7.

This ain't no joke if you think it is.

yours untruly,
A loyal RED SOX fan

P.S. You may think this is a joke or not think anything of it but you'll wish you had thought of it you better tell casey to keep you out of the game it would be better if you didn't bring your damned team to boston.

The Yanks did come to Boston, along with Mantle. The series was played with extra Boston security personnel diligently patroling the stands at Fenway. There was no incident.

Phil Rizzuto recalls another assassination threat that had almost comic overtones. "It was the year I won the MVP award. Some crank letter I had gotten was turned over to the FBI. They said if I set foot in Fenway Park somebody was going to shoot me with a high-powered rifle.

"Stengel said, 'We don't want Rizzuto shot.' So they switched uniforms with Billy Martin and me. It was a very exciting game for me, but it was even more exciting for Billy. I felt much more relaxed, but Billy never sat still for one single second. I never saw him move about so much in my life. He didn't want them to have a standing-still target."

The incident took place as the Yankees went into Boston for the final three games of the 1950 season. Rizzuto was only one hit shy of 200 for the year. The Scooter, who claims he always hit well at Fenway ("at least one of my four homers each year was there") singled in the first inning for his 200th hit of 1950. And then Stengel took the little shortstop out of the game.

Charles Dillon Stengel began his baseball career in 1910 with the Maysville, Kentucky, team in the Blue Grass League. And to have seen him then, no one would have predicted the greatness that awaited him in the future. Possessed of a predilection for loud ties that he wore along with his baseball uniform, Casey used to practice his sliding skills as he trotted out to take up his position in the outfield. Across from the Maysville ballpark was an insane asylum. Some of Casey's greatest fans were the inmates of that asylum, who used to roar with delight when they saw him practice his sliding techniques. Stengel's manager was not as delighted with his outfielder's antics. Tapping his head and pointing to the asylum, Casey's manager used to say: "For you to wind up there—it's only a matter of time."

"Fired oftener than an old target-practice pistol"—to use his own phrase—Casey took a circuitous path through baseball, by way of the Brooklyn Dodgers, Pittsburgh Pirates, Philadelphia Phillies, New York Giants, Boston Bees, and Toledo in the American Association.

Three sparkling seasons (1946–1948) managing Oakland in the Pacific Coast League led him to the New York Yankees.

He looked like a shaggy St. Bernard dog and he spoke in scrambled syntax, but old Casey could handle people and manage players. Stengel led the Yankees to an unprecedented five straight pennants and world championships (1949–1953).

"They loved him in Boston," notes Bill Crowley, "and they hated him for winning so much against the Sox. Tom Yawkey had high regard for Stengel, and whenever the Yankees came to Fenway, Mr. Yawkey used to also place a bottle of booze in Casey's locker."

Stengel loved an audience, even if it was a hostile one, and he rarely turned down an invitation to speak, even if it was before Sox diehards. At one of these speaking engagements, a Boston fan suggested that perhaps it would be best for baseball if the Yankees were broken up, for they seemed to be winning too often.

"Why is everyone mad at us?" Stengel snapped. "What do they expect us to do, roll over and play dead? Draw up a chair and sit by the roadside until the rest catch up? If you ran a delicatessen store, you would want it to be the best delicatessen store, wouldn't you? Well, that's how I feel about the Yankees."

Caught in the media's eye, framed in memory, the stark image-contrasts of the Yanks and Sox going at each other produce a special type of mood. It seems everyone has an insight, a different perspective.

"I didn't even know there was a big rivalry until I came to the Red Sox," notes Don Zimmer, "but I found out soon enough. I was coaching at third base in 1974 at Yankee Stadium, and the fans were throwing so much crap on the field that I had to put on a helmet for protection. The players don't really hate each other. It's a rivalry of fans."

Goose Gossage, star Yankee relief pitcher, recalls, "When I first came to the Yankees, the guys said you won't believe this series, you won't believe the people, the way the two teams go at each other. In late June of 1978 I made my first appearance against the Red Sox. I was all psyched up. The first game of that series was like the World Series. I wanted to go out there and kick the hell out of them."

Chico Walker is a newcomer to the rivalry, an infielder who joined the Sox in 1980. The rivalry is an important part of his professional life. "It goes back to when I broke in in rookie ball," says Walker. "Every time we played the Yankee teams, the manager would try and get us up for that. From rookie ball to Double A to Triple A, I felt it. Everyone in the Red Sox organization is pumped up playing against the New York Yankees."

Mike Torrez moved as a free agent from the Yankees to the Red Sox. Bob Watson moved as a free agent from the Red Sox to the Yankees. Both have special feelings about the rivalry, special insights they feel comfortable articulating.

"I actually became aware of the rivalry when I played for Baltimore," says Torrez, "but you had to put on the uniform to really feel it. When I was with the Yankees, the players on that team really hated the Boston players. Today, it's not so much of a hate, but you just try and beat their asses. We want to beat the Yankees bad, and I'm sure they want to beat us bad, and both teams talk

Bob Watson, pictured here in a New York Yankee uniform, played for Boston and thus has been on both sides of the rivalry

about it. Fans talk about it and they anticipate something bad happening because of all the history of violence."

Watson wanted to stay on with Boston but notes that "the management at that time did not have me in their plans." The powerful first baseman played a half-season for the Sox. "Even though I was there for just a short time, I got to see that Boston fans are probably per capita the most knowledgeable fans in all of baseball. They voted me the Tenth Player award and that will always have a special place in my heart. The rivalry is something that I can really appreciate, having been on both teams. When the two clubs meet it gives the players and the fans a chance to talk about the old times . . . when the Yankees came in and did this . . . when the Red Sox were able to do this and that. It's a good thing for all of baseball."

Torrez agrees with Watson. "There's all those past memories," he says, "that players and fans talk about and feel. That's good, but there's also that violence that's part of the past and who's to say those things could not flare up again? The 'Boston Sucks' signs don't bother me as long as they don't get physical. However, some things have been thrown from the upper deck at Yankee Stadium, and everyone is aware of that. You kind of hide your head in the dugout when you come in there. It's good you've got the concrete above you in case something does come flying down."

Frank Messer joined the Yankees as an announcer in 1968. "I became really impressed by the intensity of the rivalry. It's the two teams going at each other that makes for the excitement. People get worn out with excitement watching them play. I would hate to do a bad job broadcasting a Yankee–Red Sox game, for all of those games are something special."

A New Englander all his life, Wynn Bates lives in Braintree, Massachusetts, and is a sportswriter for the *Brockton Enterprise.* He has studied baseball's greatest rivalry for years as a New Englander and as a reporter. "Baseball is the king of all sports out here in Boston," notes Bates. "And the Yankee–Red Sox competition is the big story. No matter where the teams are in the standings, Fenway Park is always crowded for games between the rivals. If there's a tight pennant race, you can't get a ticket. People here really want to beat the Yankees. Maybe it's the animosity some in New England feel toward the city of New York. There's an uptight attitude. Sometimes Sox fans get a little out of hand. The atmosphere can be scary, especially when Yankee fans stand up and root at Fenway, and that gets some violence going."

A neutral among the partisans is Ron Luciano. He watched the rivalry play out for 11 seasons from within his American League umpire's uniform. Today he calls them as he sees them as an NBC-TV baseball announcer. Luciano has a double perspective.

"As an umpire," notes Luciano, "you play on the crowd. If you're at Fenway Park with 35,000 or at the Stadium with 45,000, 50,000—your adrenaline is up. You're always looking for strange things to happen.

"Notoriously, over the years there have been throwing incidents, there've been fights, there've been runners running into catchers at home plate. The time Reggie was pulled off the field by Billy Martin was during a Red Sox series. Some might say the rivalry did not have anything to do with it, but I think it did. The rivalry got to be so much that Martin was upset that everyone wasn't pulling two hundred percent. The rivalry is so intense that everyone plays just a bit harder. It's a bigger letdown for the Yankees to lose to Boston, and umpires feel that before they walk out there and this is passed along among umpires.

"Fans," continues Luciano, "react more to the umpires in a Boston–New York series. If one calls a foul ball and Rice is at bat against the Yankees, the umpire has to watch his life afterwards walking out of the ballpark. Boston–New York is a do-harder thing. You want to do your best in those games. It's a bargaining point. Umpires going in to talk next year's contract use it as a bargaining point. 'Hey,' they say, 'I had the Yankees and the Red Sox. You wanted your best up there in that crucial series. Reward me. I worked baseball's best rivalry."

As an announcer, Luciano views the rivalry from another vantage point. "You know that every player down there is going to try a little harder because of the rivalry and the crowd reaction. Even if they're both in last place the rivalry is still there. Everybody builds it up: the newspapers, the cameras, the players themselves—but it should be that way. It's a whole regional competition between two great cities and two great organizations."

The rivalry is Boo and Bucky and Butch. It is Carl Yastrzemski trotting out to left field at Fenway with cotton sticking out of his ears to muffle the boos of disheartened Sox fans. It is the Scooter, the Monster and the Hawk. It is Rich McKinney on April 22, 1972, making four errors on ground balls to third base that figured in

Boston's scoring of nine runs to defeat the Yankees, 11–7. It is Joe Dee and the Thumper, Yaz and the Commerce Comet, Mombo and King Kong. The rivalry is Mantle slugging a 440-foot double at Yankee Stadium in 1958 and tipping his cap to the Red Sox bench. It's George Herman Ruth. It's Williams spitting, Jackson gesturing, Martin punching, Fisk's headaches from tension coming into Yankee Stadium and Mickey Rivers' jumping out of the way of an exploding firecracker thrown into the visitors' dugout at F.P.

The rivalry is signs:

"I LOVE NEW YORK, TOO,
IT'S THE YANKEES I HATE."

"BOSTON CHOKES, BOSTON SUCKS, BOSTON DOES IT IN STYLE."

ROOTS

The Boston Red Sox came into existence in 1901 and remained one of the most successful of all baseball franchises through the first 19 years of the team's existence. By 1918, they had won six pennants and five World Series. The New York Highlanders (they officially became the Yankees in 1913) were a sad counterpoint to the attractive and glamorous Sox. In their first 16 years, the New Yorkers finished under .500 eight times, and last in the league twice.

After the Red Sox won the 1916 World Series, Harry Frazee, a former Peoria, Illinois, billposter, purchased the club from Joe Lannin. All agreed that the future looked bright for Frazee and the Red Sox. The pitching staff included Dutch Leonard, Carl Mays and Ernie Shore; a young phenom named George Herman Ruth was also on the club. The outfield was golden—Tris Speaker, Harry Hooper and Duffy Lewis. The rest of the supporting cast fit in quite well.

"Nothing is too good," declared Frazee, who hadn't even paid Lannin for the purchase of the Sox, "for the wonderful fans of the Boston team." Hub zealots should have taken Frazee at his word. For as the future was to show, Frazee meant exactly what he said.

A show business wheeler-dealer who owned a theater on 42nd Street in Manhattan, close by the Yankee offices, Frazee was a gambler. And he was always scuffling about for a buck, always overextended in one theatrical deal or another.

The World War I era negatively affected Boston's attendance, and the war economy hindered some of Frazee's show business ventures. Hurting in the pocketbook, Frazee looked to the New York Yankees for a silver lining. He dispatched pitchers Ernie Shore and Dutch Leonard and outfielder Duffy Lewis to the Bronx Bombers four days before Christmas, 1918. Frazee netted $50,-000 for the trio—a nice Christmas present.

The next installment in Frazee's follies involved Carl Mays. A submarine-ball hurler, Mays had back-to-back 20-win seasons in 1917–1918 for the Red "Sawks." By midseason of 1919, his won and lost record was 5–11. His attitude was as depressed as his record.

"I'm going fishing," he snapped on July 13, blaming his poor fortune on his teammates' inept fielding skills. Mays followed this statement with another and more definitive one a couple of days later. "I hate the Boston team. I'll never pitch another game for the Red Sox again."

Frazee had no part in May's malaise, but he was not one to let an opportunity to make an extra buck pass him by. A good friend of Yankee owners Colonel Jacob Ruppert and Colonel Tillinghast l'Hommedieu Huston, Frazee started wheeling and dealing again with the rich New Yorkers who had purchased the club in 1915 and were highly motivated to produce the first New York Yankee championship team.

On July 29, 1919, two weeks after Mays "jumped" the Boston team, he was shipped to New York for $40,000 and pitchers Allan Russell and Bob McGraw. All of baseball, and especially Boston, was in an uproar.

American League president Ban Johnson announced, "Baseball cannot tolerate such a breach of discipline. It was up to the owners of the Boston club to suspend Carl Mays for breaking his contract and when they failed to do so it is my duty as head of the American League to act. Mays will not play with any club until the suspension is raised. He should have reported to the Boston club before they made any trade or sale." The Johnson proclamation was followed by a lawsuit and a counter lawsuit and increasing controversy. In the end Mays, like Leonard, Shore and Lewis before him—and many after him—became a Yankee. In 1921 the Yankees won 98 games and their first pennant. Mays chipped in with 27 victories.

Boston fans were alarmed at the loss of Mays to the Yankees, but what lay in store for them would give them fits.

George Herman Ruth was born in Baltimore in 1894. When he was eight years old he was placed in St. Mary's

The Babe—Boston's loss and New York's gain

Industrial School for Boys, an institution noted for its treatment of "incorrigible behavior." It was at St. Mary's that Ruth learned how to play baseball.

When he was 16, he was permitted to leave St. Mary's and become a member of the Baltimore Orioles baseball team. A phenomenal pitcher and power hitter, Ruth was purchased by the Red Sox in 1914. He was an 18-game winner in 1915, a 23-game winner in 1916, a 24-game winner in 1917. With each passing season of success as a hurler, Ruth was given more and more time to ply his trade as a slugging outfielder. In 1918 he batted 317 times and tied for the league lead in home runs, with 11.

Frazee was thrilled with the all-around accomplishments of his slugger-hurler. Ruth was not enamored with the salary he was drawing—$7,000. He told Frazee at the end of the 1918 season that he wanted a two-year contract for at least $12,000 a season. Frazee refused.

Ruth told reporters that if he did not receive what he thought was his due, he would quit baseball. The Babe claimed he would be quite happy to retire to his farm in suburban Massachusetts and lavish his attention on his 20 head of cattle, his three dozen pigs, his scores of hens, his three horses and his Collie dog, "Dixie."

Frazee implied that Ruth was simply "whistling Dixie," and announced that he would not give in to the "absurd salary demands." That winter of 1919 Ruth escalated his demands. He claimed that he was fed up with platooning as a pitcher and outfielder.

"I want to be a regular player," snapped Ruth. "I'll win more games playing in the outfield than I will pitching every fourth day and everybody knows that."

The 1919 baseball schedule was reduced to 140 games

because of the repercussions of the end of World War I. The Red Sox were scheduled in mid-March to go by steamer to spring training in Florida. They had abandoned their Hot Springs, Arkansas, site in order to play a series of exhibition games with the Giants of John McGraw and then barnstorm north. Ruth was still holding out, and all knew that without him much of the glitter of the Red Sox would be missing from the tour.

Frazee and Ruth met in Manhattan on March 21. The meeting place was Frazee's office, the walls of which were adorned with posters and photographs that depicted shows Frazee had produced. There were autographed pictures of Eddie Foy, George M. Cohan, the Barrymores—Frazee's show business friends. Ruth kidded with secretaries and signed autographs before entering Frazee's private office.

"I want ten thousand dollars a year for three years," Ruth told Frazee, not wasting any time, "and I want to play the outfield full time."

Frazee grabbed at his chest, almost dropping the pen he held in his hand in anticipation of the Babe's signing a contract. "You've gotta be nuts," he screamed at the Babe. "I don't even pay my stage fellows that kind of money."

"What the fuck do I care about actors?" screamed Ruth. "I'll be a bigger star one day than every God damned one of them. All I want is my God damned money, and I tell you, Frazee, I'll hold out for the entire season if I don't get it! I want what I'm telling you or I don't play for you!"

Ruth got what he wanted. Frazee was disgusted but able to recognize the star status of the Babe. "Besides,"

Frazee said later, "how the hell could you argue with someone like Ruth, who had no respect for the acting profession."

In 1919, Frazee and baseball fans got their money's worth. Ruth batted .322 and set a new major league mark for home runs in a season—29. It was a mark many thought would last forever. The Babe also recorded 139 hits—75 for extra bases, including 34 doubles and 12 triples. These impressive statistics had been compiled in just 432 at-bats in 130 games. But even with Ruth, the drab Red Sox finished in sixth place and drew just 417,291 fans into Fenway Park.

On January 9, 1920, what would become known as "Harry Frazee's Crime" was enacted. At a cold morning news conference, Colonel Jacob Ruppert announced, "Gentlemen, we have just bought Babe Ruth from Harry Frazee of the Boston Red Sox. I can't give exact figures, but it was a pretty check—six figures. No players are involved. It was strictly a cash deal."

For Frazee, it was the only way to retain control of the Sox. He received $100,000 cash, a guaranteed $350,000 mortgage on Fenway Park and the promise of more money for more players if needed.

News of the sale of Babe Ruth sent shock waves throughout New England. Frazee was hung in effigy. He was called "Hairbreadth Harry" and choicer things. "Ruth's 29 home runs," said Frazee, rationalizing his move, "were more spectacular than useful. They didn't help the Red Sox get out of sixth place." To intimates, Frazee was more honest. "I can't help it," he said. "I'm up against the wall. Joe Lannin was starting to call in his mortgage on Fenway Park. I need money desperately."

Ruth was at first shaken and annoyed that he was going to the Yankees. "My heart is in Boston," he told reporters. "I have a farm in Sudbury. I like New England." In New York City, John McGraw of the Giants gritted his teeth and prepared for the attendance battle he knew was looming ahead. The peppery Giant manager could sense the gate potential of Babe Ruth.

The dark age of Boston baseball can be traced directly to the sale of Babe Ruth to the Yankees. The golden age of Yankee baseball can be traced directly to their acquisition of the Bambino. And the animosity, the ill feelings, the combative atmosphere that still characterize Red Sox–Yankee competition have much to do with the Frazee shuttle of players to New York. Up until the sale of Ruth, the Red Sox were one of the most successful of all baseball franchises. With the coming of Ruth, the Yankees became baseball's most successful team.

Comfortably clothed in pinstripes, with a guaranteed salary of $20,000 a year for his first two seasons, Ruth did not miss Boston and missed Frazee even less. "That Frazee was a cheap son of a bitch," the Babe snarled. "They had a Babe Ruth Day for me last year [1919] and I had to buy my wife tickets to the game. Fifteen thousand fans showed up and all I got was a cigar."

The money the Yankees paid for Babe Ruth was money well spent. In 1920 he slammed 54 home runs, batted .376, drove in 137 runs. He led the league in runs scored (158), stolen bases (14), slugging percentage (.847). The name and face of Babe Ruth became known to more people in the United States than those of any other player in baseball. Writers overreached straining to characterize the phenomenal slugger. He was called "Sultan of Swat,"

"Wizard of Whack," "Goliath of Grand Slams," "Prince of Pounders," "Behemoth of Biff," "Infant Swatagy."

The Yankees of 1920 finished in third place, two notches ahead of the struggling Red Sox. In 1919, without Ruth, the Yanks drew 619,614. With Ruth acting like a magnet at the turnstiles, the 1920 Yankees attracted 1,289,444—an attendance record that stood until 1946.

Boston general manager Ed Barrow, who had felt that Ruth's best position was pitcher but was proven wrong, and who had fought against the sale of the Babe to the Yankees but was outvoted, followed the path of so many other Red Sox to New York. He parted company with Frazee on October 29, 1920, a year after Ruth. Joining the Bronx Bombers as general manager, he would now be on the receiving end of the Boston–New York shuttle instead of on the sending side.

On December 15, 1920, Barrow and the Yankees received Waite Hoyt and Harry Harper, catcher Wally Schang and third baseman Mike McNally. The Red Sox acquired outfielder Sam Vick, who played right field before Ruth joined New York, catcher Muddy Ruel and second baseman Derrill Pratt. The Red Sox also received cash. The key figure in the multiple-player trade was pitcher Waite Hoyt. Just 6–6 with Boston in 1919, he won 19 games in each of the next two seasons on his way to a place in the Hall of Fame.

With each new deal, the Yankees grew stronger and the Red Sox grew weaker. And Boston fans grew more vociferous in their protests. "Who did Frazz sell today?" was the question asked throughout New England. Telegrams were sent to Commissioner Landis objecting to the "rape of the Red Sox."

When Jake Ruppert had purchased 50 percent of the Yankees on January 11, 1915, he was convinced that the team would be a good vehicle to aid his beer company sales. Rebuffed by the 13 managing editors of New York City newspapers who voted against his proposal to change the name of the team to Knickerbockers, after the name of his best-selling beer, Ruppert vowed that he'd find another way to make the team pay for itself—by winning on the field. By tapping the Frazee pipeline of Sox stars, Ruppert kept his vow.

The 1921 Yankees won 98 games and lost 55 and won their first American League pennant, by 4½ games over the Cleveland Indians (who had seven regulars who batted .310 or more). Boston finished in fifth place, 23½ games off the pace. Managed by tiny Miller Huggins, with Ed Barrow as general manager, the Yanks had a decided Red Sox flavor.

Babe Ruth was very close to peak form. He slashed 59 home runs, drove in 171 runs and batted .378. Catcher Wally Schang chipped in with a .316 batting average. Mike McNally was the regular third baseman. Carl Mays, who hadn't wanted to pitch for the Red Sox, was the workhorse of the Yankee staff. He appeared in more games (49), pitched more innings (337) and won more games (27) than any other pitcher in the league. And Waite Hoyt, a six-game winner for Boston in 1920, won 19 for New York in 1921.

The World Series was all New York—the Giants against the Yankees. Despite the herculean efforts of Waite Hoyt (27 innings pitched and no runs allowed) the Yanks lost the Series to the Giants. Miller Huggins told Ruppert, "We could have won if we had more pitching."

In December 1921, Ruppert and his good friend Frazee got together. Huggins was elated. Sox fans were livid. Frazee shipped his 1921 pitching aces Bullet Joe Bush and Sad Sam Jones to the Yanks along with shortstop Everett Scott. Former Yankee captain-shortstop Roger Peckinpaugh plus pitchers Bill Piercy and Jack Quinn moved on to Boston.

Peckinpaugh was perhaps the most valuable player that Frazee acquired in the trade for the pitching aces Bush and Jones, but Peckinpaugh was a member of the Red Sox for just one day. For cash and "Jumping Joe" Dugan, Frazee peddled Peckinpaugh to the Washington Senators.

In midsummer 1922, Dugan was playing a steady game at shortstop for the Sox and batting .287. The Yankees were involved in a tough pennant fight and had a gap at third base. Ruppert's solution was to turn to his "Boston farm team." Dugan and outfielder Elmer Smith were dispatched to the Yankees for pitcher Lefty O'Doul, a couple of no-name players and cash. There was always *cash,* even though all the Boston–New York trades were announced with the tag line, "There were no other considerations."

With Dugan shoring up the infield, the 1922 Yankees won their second straight pennant, edging out the St. Louis Browns by one game. Hoyt, Jones, Bush and Mays—the escapees from Boston—combined to win 71 games. The Red Sox finished in last place, 33 games out.

Once again the Yankees faced the Giants in the World Series and once again the Giants were the victors, sweeping the Yanks in four straight. The Bronx Bombers had strong pitching arms—Mays, Bush, Jones, etc.—but they were all right-handers. Huggins once again approached Ruppert with a request to strengthen the Yankees. "We could win the whole thing," he said, "if we could only pick up a strong left-handed pitcher." Ruppert told his little manager, "I'll see what I can do."

When the 1922 season ended, *Reach's Baseball Guide* for 1923 commented that "Boston last season reached the fruits of four years' despoliation by the New York club, and for the second time in American League baseball history, this once great Boston team, now utterly discredited, fell into last place, with every prospect of remaining in that undesirable position indefinitely."

It was that "discredited" club that Colonel Jake Ruppert surveyed, looking for a southpaw pitcher. Like a vulture, the Yankees had picked the Boston roster clean over the years. There was not much left, but there was a left-hander named Herb Pennock, the "Squire of Kennett Square." Pennock had won but ten games in 1922, against 17 losses, but most baseball experts agreed that with a good team behind him he would be an effective pitcher.

Ruppert made his deal with Frazee. The Yankees obtained Pennock, a ten-year veteran, and George Pipgras, a player of promise. Boston received pitcher Norman McMillan, pitcher George Murray, outfielder Camp Skinner and *cash*. Pennock went on to post a 19–6 record for the 1923 Yankees and to add class and leadership to the team for the next 11 years.

The Pennock trade was made on January 30, 1923, just about the time that over 950,000 board-feet of Pacific Coast fir was brought through the Panama Canal for the erection of the bleachers in the new ballpark that Ruppert was constructing, to be known as Yankee Stadium.

Tenants at the Polo Grounds since April 1913, the Yankees had been bluntly informed that they should look around for a new playing field. The magnetic gate appeal of Babe Ruth and other stars had become an embarrassment to the Giants, who were being outdrawn in their own ballpark.

Beer baron Ruppert acquired the land across the Harlem River from the Polo Grounds at the mouth of a stream called Crowell's Creek. On May 22, 1922, the White Construction Company was given the contract to build a stadium to house the Yankees.

In less than nine months, on 240,000 square feet of land that had once been part of the estate of millionaire William Waldorf Astor, over the completely filled-in bed of Crowell's Creek, construction crews labored to erect the stadium out of steel and reinforced concrete. The park was both a monument to Yankee success and a footnote to Boston's decline.

Yankee Stadium was both the "House That Ruth Built" and the "House Built for Ruth." Its dimensions provoked much controversy, tailored as they were for Ruth's left-handed power. The right-field fence was just 296 feet away along the foul line extension, and 367 feet to dead right field. Just 43 inches high, the fence was the lowest in the majors.

Yankee Stadium seated 20,000 more than any other park of its time. It was also the first triple-decked structure known to baseball. A dull-green, oval-shaped facility, it was a place where the late afternoon's sun would shape strange mosaic designs on the center-field grass and hamper the vision of the outfielders.

A gigantic horseshoe shaped by the triple-decked

grandstands arching into foul territory off the line of left field behind home plate and then out to the right field line, the park was a cathedral of baseball. Huge wooden bleachers circled the park, And the 10,712 upper grandstand seats and 14,543 lower grandstand seats were sturdily fixed in place by 135,000 individual steel castings on which 400,000 pieces of maple lumber were fastened by over a million screws.

Dead center field was 461 feet from home plate and was referred to as Death Valley. Behind first base ran East 157th Street. Ruppert Place was located behind third base. In back of left field was 161st Street, and River Avenue was behind right field. In the beams and rafters of the park, vast numbers of pigeons resided. Fat from the peanuts and popcorn that spilled out in the aisles, the pigeons would bolt into flight at the noise of huge crowds leaping to their feet to cheer a big play.

The first game at Yankee Stadium was played on April 18, 1923. Thousands trundled up the ramps of the triple-tiered park. Many of the record 76,217 in attendance wore dinner jackets, heavy sweaters, coats, hats. The temperature at game time was a chilly 49 degrees, and the wind whipped at the Yankee pennants and blew about clouds of dust from the dirt roads that led to the stadium. More than 25,000 lingered outside the park, unable to gain entrance to the jammed facility but excited by the proudest moment in the history of the South Bronx.

Commissioner Kenesaw Mountain Landis, Colonel Jacob Ruppert and Governor Al Smith were seated in the celebrity box. The march beat of the band conducted by John Philip Sousa was the dominant sound.

There were many former Boston Red Sox players on

the Yankee team that faced the Philadelphia Athletics. Babe Ruth and catcher Wally Schang and third baseman Joe Dugan and shortstop Everett Scott were in the starting lineup.

In the third inning, Ruth came to bat against Howard Ehmke with two men on base. With the count 2–2, Ehmke attempted to fool Ruth with a slow pitch. Ruth hammered it on a line and the ball jumped, rising as it streaked to the outfield and finally coming to rest in the right-field bleachers. The huge crowd was on its feet roaring as Ruth crossed home plate. He paused. He removed his cap, extended it out in front of him at arm's length and waved it to the cheering multitude.

Before the game, Ruth had told reporters, "I'd give a year of my life if I can hit a home run in this first game in this new park." Ruth got his wish and the Yankees, behind veteran Bob Shawkey's three-hitter, defeated the A's, 4–1. The total attendance of 76,217 broke the previous record of 42,000, set in a World Series game at Boston.

In July 1923, after 7½ years of diminishing returns, Harry Frazee sold out as owner of the Red Sox. Free to concentrate on his "real love," the theater, Frazee went on to make a fortune on Broadway as the producer of *No No Nanette* and other musicals. Back in Boston, virtually every player on the defending champion team he had purchased had been traded or sold—most of them to the Yankees, who that season were rolling to their third straight pennant and their first world championship.

Robert "Bob" Quinn, former vice-president and general manager of the St. Louis Browns, and millionaire Winslow Palmer became the new owners of the Red Sox.

Quinn energetically attempted to revive the franchise but ran into a series of bad breaks. Palmer, counted on to bankroll the Sox, died less than two years after the team was purchased. Then the years of the Great Depression eroded extra cash that Boston fans would have expended on the team. There was also what was known as "Quinn's Weather." Inclement atmospheric conditions seemed to be always plaguing the Sox. "Every time we get set for a big crowd," sighed Quinn, "it seems to rain."

While Quinn struggled with the weather, Ruppert's Yankees just sailed along, first class all the way. In 1930, Ruppert signed a three-year contract to quarter the Yanks at the Don CeSar Hotel during spring training. Dubbed the "pink palace" because of its magnificent Spanish architecture and pink color, the luxury hotel is still in its original location—21 miles west of Tampa, Florida, on the Gulf of Mexico.

The arrangement was a good deal for the hotel management—a guaranteed sell-out for three seasons. For Ruppert, the arrangement was a bargain. Room rates were eight dollars per person, double occupancy, including meals. Ruppert was also assured that his players would be served steak for breakfast along with unlimited quantities of milk each morning. Thus, the Yankee owner was able to clinch a good start for his club each season courtesy of the Don CeSar deal that provided lavish lodgings, fine food, fresh air. And perhaps the best part of the arrangement was that Colonel Ruppert was able to keep his charges away from the "flesh pots" of St. Petersburg. The only Yankee who did not stay at the Don CeSar was Babe Ruth. He preferred St. Petersburg.

On May 6, 1930, feeling the financial squeeze that had

seized Frazee, Quinn followed Frazee's time-worn path. He traded pitcher Red Ruffing to the New York Yankees for outfielder Cedric Durst and $50,000.

Durst was 34 years old and in six previous seasons had never performed in more than 92 games a campaign. The 1930 season was his last—he batted .240, four points below his lifetime average. Ruffing was 15–5 for the 1930 Yanks in the seventh year of a 22-season Hall of Fame career. The Durst-Ruffing deal was just more salt on the raw wound in the Sox-Yankee rivalry.

In 1933, Thomas Austin Yawkey purchased the Boston Red Sox. A nephew of the late Bill Yawkey, one-time owner of the Detroit Tigers, he had come into the bulk of a huge financial-estate trust fund and was prepared to spend much of it to make the Sox into winners. In the dozen years before the coming of Yawkey, Boston had become the street urchin of the American League. Nine times it had finished in last place, and Fenway Park was a dilapidated, downtrodden slum. In that same time period the Yankees in their glittering new park had recorded seven pennants.

Yawkey spent $750,000 reconstructing Fenway Park in 1934 and $250,000 to acquire player-manager Joe Cronin from Washington in what was the second biggest baseball deal to that point in time. Cronin, the 28-year-old son-in-law of Washington owner Clark Griffith, was installed as Sox shortstop and manager in 1935, and for the first time since 1918 and the days of Ed Barrow, Boston played over .500 ball, finishing in fourth place, 16 games out of first.

The mortgage was even paid off on Fenway Park ahead of schedule as a result of some unexpected Red Sox suc-

Boston's pride—player-manager Joe Cronin, who went on to become the team's general manager and then American League president

cess on the playing field. When Yawkey had acquired the Sox, arrangements were made between him and Ruppert to carry the Frazee demand mortgage through the 1934 season. In 1933, however, the Sox swept the Yanks in five games at Fenway. Ruppert was furious. "It was a costly sweep," recalled Yawkey. "Ruppert demanded immediate payment on the mortgage." Yawkey paid immediately, severing forever any financial linkage and leverage between the two teams.

Yawkey always had a quick pen and a ready checkbook. Intent on making the Sox into a contender, he picked up stars from other teams—Lefty Grove, Max Bishop, Heinie Manush, Rube Walberg, Jimmie Foxx.

Boston finished in sixth place in 1936, in fifth place in 1937. There were back-to-back second-place finishes in 1938–1939 behind the Yankees. And in July 1939 one of the most satisfying moments in the rivalry for Boston fans took place as the Sox swept the Yanks in five straight games at Yankee Stadium, chopping New York's 11½-game lead to 6½. "Just who the hell are supposed to be the world champions," screamed an irate Yankee manager Joe McCarthy. "Us or the damn Red Sox? We're a whole lot better than Boston." Agonizing as it was for Sox rooters, McCarthy was right. In 1942, Boston finished in second place—the fourth time in five seasons that the Red Sox finished second behind the Yankees.

The war years had great impact on baseball and the rest of the world, but Tom Yawkey would still pursue his dream of beating out the hated foe, the New York Yankees.

"Ruppert bought some pennants when he was able to reach out to the Red Sox for players," said Yawkey. "It doesn't seem to work for us when we buy old champions. So we've got to do something else and raise our own. We've got to build up a farm system such as Rickey has built in St. Louis and Barrow and Weiss in New York. That's the only way we can catch the Yankees."

Yawkey and the Red Sox attempted to catch up, but the Yankees, with George Weiss on the scene, were forging ahead. Some say Weiss not only copied Branch Rickey's farm system concept, he improved on it. Yankee farm teams were organized all over the United States: Kansas City; Butler, Pennsylvania; Norfolk, Virginia; Springfield, Massachusetts; Augusta, Georgia; Akron; Bassett, Virginia; Beaumont, Texas. The glittering jewel of the Yankee organization was at Newark, New Jersey, where from 1932 to 1938 the Bears racked up five first-place finishes. In 1937, the club posted a 109–43 record; 16 of its 17 regulars became major league players.

A short, dour man, Weiss pursued excellence with frugality and passion. From 1932 to 1943, Yankee teams recorded eight pennants with players mainly produced from the farm system. Only $100,000 was spent for five player purchases. One of those purchased cost $25,000. His name was Joe DiMaggio.

JOE AND TED

Perhaps no two players have symbolized the Yankee–Red Sox rivalry as much as Joe DiMaggio and Ted Williams. Both Californians, they found stardom in the East. Both bigger than life, they seemed sculpted into their respective superstar roles. One was an outspoken iconoclast, the other a soft-spoken team man.

Born November 25, 1914, at Martinez, California, Joseph Paul DiMaggio was one of nine children of a fisherman father who had emigrated from Sicily. It was all planned for Joe to become a fisherman like his father, but Joe could not abide the smell of fish and he often got seasick. His real passion was playing baseball.

In 1934, Joe DiMaggio was purchased from the San Francisco Seals in the Pacific Coast League. "Getting him," general manager George Weiss was fond of saying, "was the greatest thing I ever did for the Yankees." The price for DiMaggio was $25,000 and five minor-league players. The deal also contained the condition that the graceful outfielder be allowed to play one more season for San Francisco. DiMaggio's 1935 season for the Seals gave the city of San Francisco something to remember. He batted .398, recorded 270 hits, drove in 154 runs.

Permission was granted in 1936 for DiMaggio to drive cross-country with fellow San Franciscans Tony Lazzeri and Frank Crosetti to the Yankee spring training camp at St. Petersburg, Florida. Reportedly, Lazzeri turned to DiMaggio after the trio had concluded one day of driving and said, "You take over, Joe."

"I don't drive," DiMaggio answered. It was reported that these were the only words he uttered during the entire three-day California-to-Florida journey.

In 1935, Ted Williams was a pitcher-outfielder at Herbert Hoover High School in his native San Diego. He batted .586. His mother, an ardent Salvation Army worker, thought he was worth a $1,000 bonus for signing with a major league team. Bill Essick, a scout for the Yankees, listened, thought and finally decided that Williams was not worth that much money. "I don't know whether one thousand dollars stood between me being a Yank or not," Williams recalled. "There were those who said years later 'You will regret not having been a Yankee. You would be a great hero in New York. Yankee Stadium was built for a left-handed batter.' "

Williams signed with San Diego in the Pacific Coast League. He played in 42 games in 1936 and the following season batted .291 and recorded 23 home runs. The manager of the Boston Bees in the National League, a humorous gent named Casey Stengel, observed Williams playing for San Diego. He recommended that the Boston team sign the youngster. The Bees' management decided that the asking price was too high. The other Boston team, the Red Sox, thought the price was right and signed Williams.

When the 6'3", curly-haired Williams arrived at the Red Sox spring training camp in 1938, he noticed that all the team's stars were from someplace else: Joe Cronin was from Washington, Doc Cramer was from Philadelphia, Joe Vosmik was from St. Louis and Ben Chapman was from Washington. Jimmy Foxx, who had starred for many years with the A's, was winding up his Hall of Fame career with the Sox.

"Ted," said Bobby Doerr, a friend of Williams from their PCL days, "wait 'til you see this guy Foxx hit."

"Bobby," snapped Williams, "wait 'til Foxx sees me hit."

Williams did not hit that well in spring training of 1938, and to the delight of some of the Red Sox stars he had alienated, he was sent down to Minneapolis of the American Association for more experience. "I'll be back," he snarled at some of the Boston stars, "and I'll be greater than you guys." In 1939 he returned. He had led the American Association in homers (43), RBIs (142), and batting average (.366) and was poised to batter American League pitching.

Ted Williams' first year with the Red Sox, 1939, was Joe DiMaggio's fourth season with the New York Yankees. In his first three seasons the Yankee Clipper had batted .323, .346, and .324 and glided about the centerfield pastureland of Yankee Stadium with a quiet ease and grace.

The Sox and Yankees went head-to-head for the pennant that year. And Williams and DiMaggio went head-to-head for the first of many seasons they would vie for the attention and admiration of fans.

Williams began his rookie season in New York. It rained for two days before he was able to play in his first game. He arrived at Yankee Stadium to play against the Yankees of Lou Gehrig, Tommy Henrich, Frank Crosetti, Bill Dickey, Charlie Keller and Joe DiMaggio. Red Ruffing, one of Harry Frazee's "gifts," was pitching for the Yankees. Williams struck out in his first two at-bats. His third time up he smashed the ball to deep right-center field. It missed going into the bleachers by inches, and Williams wound up on second base with a double. It was the first of what would be 2,654 major league hits—and it came against the Yankees.

Williams batted .327 in his rookie season. He recorded 31 home runs, drove in 145 and formed a potent partnership with Foxx, who batted .360 and lashed 35 home runs. DiMag prevailed over both of them. Batting a league-leading .381, the quiet Yankee drove in 126 runs and rapped out 30 homers. Both Williams and DiMaggio were named to the All-Star team—the first of six times they played together. The Yankee Clipper earned the first of his three Most Valuable Player awards. That was how the Williams-DiMaggio competition began, and throughout their careers the comparisons would come in cascades.

DiMaggio would step into the batter's box and stub his right toe into the dirt in back of his left heel. It was almost a dance step. His feet were spaced approximately four feet apart, with the weight of his frame on his left leg. Erect, almost in a military position, Joe Dee would hold his bat at the end and poise it on his right shoulder—a rifle at the ready. He would look out at the pitcher from deep in the batter's box and assume a stance that almost crowded the plate. Without a bat and with his left arm extended straight out, "standing in the batter's box," observed writer Tom Meany, "Joe DiMaggio with his right hand cocked close to the breast looked like an old boxing print of John L. Sullivan."

Williams was a contrasting image. Left-handed, "loose as a goose," in the phrase of some fans, he stood at the plate wiggling and waggling the bat. His eyes were everywhere, checking the pitcher, the fielders, the wind, the plate. He seemed to be possessed by a nervous twitch, driven to hit the ball if it was a strike. "Ted Williams looked like the hitter on the cover on an old *Spaulding Guide*," said Casey Stengel, "but when they pitched to him everything happened in just the right way. I bet there wasn't more than a dozen times in his life when he was really fooled by pitchers."

"You could shut your eyes behind home plate when Williams was batting," says Ron Luciano. "If it was a strike, Ted would swing at it. If it was a ball, he would let it go by. He was an umpire at bat. Williams trained himself to swing at good pitches, although the opposition complained that he got four strikes."

"Joe was the complete player in everything he did," said Joe McCarthy, who managed both Williams and Di-Maggio. "They'd hit the ball to center field, and Joe would stretch out those long legs of his and run the ball down. He never made a mistake on the bases and in a tough park for a right-hander; he was a great hitter, one of the best. But, of course, there wasn't anything Williams couldn't do with a bat."

In 1941 the United States was poised on the brink of World War II. The nation was dominated by baseball news, riveted on the deeds of the Red Sox star and the Yankee hero as they went head-to-head, setting records that still stand. It was a season in which DiMaggio hit safely in 56 consecutive games, and Ted Williams became the first player to bat over .400 since Bill Terry of the New York Giants compiled a .401 average in 1930.

DiMaggio's streak began on May 15 and ended July 17. During the incredible streak that had fans—especially Yankee fans—agog with admiration, he recorded 15 home runs, four triples and 16 doubles, drove in 55 runs, scored 56 runs, and batted .408. The scoreboard operator in left field at Fenway Park would pass on the news of DiMaggio's progress during the streak to Ted Williams. And Williams would yell to Joe's brother, Dom, who played center field for the Red Sox, "Joe's just got another hit." There was a rivalry between the Sox and Yankee fans, but Williams rooted all the while for DiMag to keep the streak going. As a hitter, he could appreciate the magnitude of the accomplishment. "You can talk all you want about Hornsby's .424 average," said Williams, "and

Hack Wilson's 190 RBIs, but when DiMag hit in those 56 consecutive games, he put a line in the record book. It's the one that will never be changed."

Day after day throughout 1941, Williams pursued another record—a .400 batting average, another line in the record book that probably never will be duplicated. He leaned into pitches with that bull-whipping, elastic grace. Those pitches that were not strikes, he let go by. At one point he had a string of 36 bases on balls in 19 straight games.

There were those who said that Williams had superhuman vision. Williams had extraordinary vision, 20–10, but his excellence came from dedication. "I was a guy who practiced until the blisters bled," Williams explained. "And then I practiced some more. I lived by a book on pitchers. I honestly believe that I can recall everything there was to know about my first 300 home runs—who the pitcher was, where I hit the ball, what the score was, where I hit the pitch."

With a week left in the 1941 season, Boston manager Joe Cronin suggested that Williams sit out the remaining games to protect his average. The Thumper was batting .406. "If I'm a .400 hitter," snapped Williams, "I'm a .400 hitter for the entire season, not a part of one. I'll play out the year." Williams was batting .399 as the Sox prepared to play their final 1941 weekend series with the Philadelphia Athletics. Saturday was rainy and cold, and the game was rescheduled as part of a Sunday doubleheader.

That day was damp and dreary, and there were only 10,000 in the Philadelphia ballpark. Frankie Hayes, the A's catcher, told Williams as he came up for his first turn at bat, "If we let up on you, Mr. Mack [the A's owner-manager] said he would run us out of baseball. I wish you all the luck in the world, but we're not going to give you a damn thing."

Plate umpire Bill McGowan dusted off home plate and avoided looking at Williams. "To hit .400 a batter has got to be loose," said McGowan. "Are you loose, Ted?"

In the first game, Williams came to bat five times and stroked four hits. In the second game, Williams went two for three. It was an awesome hitting clinic. In the double-header, Williams collected six hits in eight tries, including his 37th home run. His final batting average was .406—making him the last player to date in baseball history to hit .400 in a season. Hardly anyone noticed that his slugging average was an amazing .735. Williams not only led the league in batting and slugging, he was also first in home runs, walks, runs scored and home run percentage. DiMaggio batted .357 and paced the American League in RBIs. When it came time for the Most Valuable Player award, it was Joe DiMaggio (291 votes) who was selected, not Ted Williams (254 votes.) The Yankees had won the pennant by 17 games over the second-place Red Sox, and the Yankee Clipper had batted safely in 56 straight games. That was the rationale. For Red Sox rooters, it was just a bit more salt on the wound in a rivalry that was not just New York–Boston but also Williams–DiMaggio.

That season of accomplishment accentuated the skills and the differences that made Williams and DiMaggio such contrasting personalities, such different types of ball player.

DiMag was cooperative; Williams was controversial. The Boston slugger did not care about fielding. DiMaggio's outfield skills made him the complete player. Ted hurt his team by walking too much. The Yankee Clipper was at his best in the clutch but he didn't have the sheer natural hitting power of Williams. So the debate raged.

Ted was tempestuous; Joe was dignified. Williams did not wear a tie and favored casual sports clothes. DiMaggio was always well groomed, and in 1936 was voted one of the ten best-dressed men in America. Williams was red-necked, rabbit-eared, outspoken and opinionated; a physical man, he did 50 push-ups a day, and then 50 more on his fingertips. DiMag rarely smiled, sipped his half-cups of coffee, kept his feelings inside. His exterior was placid; some said it was cold and sullen and unfeeling. Number 5 was the ultimate perfectionist, who took it very personally when the Yankees lost.

Williams was the main man of the BoSox, but DiMaggio was the Yankee Clipper. With Williams, Boston was a first-division team, a frequent contender. Without him, Boston was a second-division club, out of the money. In Ted's first two decades with the team, it finished out of the first division just three times. Each of these times Williams was in the Armed Forces. In the 11 years before DiMaggio arrived on the scene, the Yankees won only four pennants. In Joe Dee's 13 seasons with the Bronx Bombers, they won 10 pennants. In the 19 seasons that Williams played for the Red Sox, they were able to manage just one pennant.

Many viewed Boston's shortcomings and New York's success as directly attributable to Williams and DiMaggio. Sportswriter Dan Parker summed it up when he wrote

The Yankees take their cue from Joe DiMaggio. He is a true team player obsessed with winning. . . . After paying tribute to Ted's gift of meeting the ball and sending it squarely on a line, some of us have come to the conclusion that despite his tremendous batting ability, Williams is what is wrong with the Red Sox ... a team with such an outstanding star usually takes its cue from him. No one can say that Williams is a team player. His chief interest seems to be in fattening Ted Williams' batting average.

Other comparisons were drawn. Williams played at Fenway Park, a southpaw slugger handicapped by his home field, where many times the wind was blowing in. Yet, in 1,171 games he managed 1406 hits in 3903 at bats for a .360 Fenway Park lifetime average that included 248 home runs and 978 runs batted in. At Yankee Stadium, he recorded 147 hits in 476 trips to the plate while compiling a .309 average and 30 home runs. It was an admirable record, but there were many who thought that he could have done more, who were not happy with his attitude, his outspokenness, aspects of his play.

Williams was criticized for failing to run full tilt after fly balls, for seemingly leaning against an invisible fence in left field in a lazy fixed position. "They'll never get me out of a game running into a wall," snapped the man some called Terrible Ted. "I'll make a damned good try, but you can bet your sweet life I won't get killed. They don't pay off on fielding."

"I saw guys who were .220 hitters who did the same things," recalls Ted's long-time teammate Johnny Pesky, "but it was never magnified to the same extent. When you're a player of the stature that Williams was, they want you to do everything perfectly. Ted was a loafer. DiMag was a different type of person."

Joe DiMaggio's weaknesses were generally overlooked.

Ted Williams' lapses were grist for gossipy headlines. He was criticized because he didn't visit his mother often enough and because he was not present at the birth of his first child. What was overlooked were the facts that he gave much financial aid to his mother and that the birth of his daughter was a premature one.

In his second season with the Sox, Williams decided that he would not tip his cap to the fans. It was not his way. He refused to sign autographs when he wasn't in the mood. He lingered in the clubhouse hours after a game to safeguard his privacy—as did DiMag. He managed a draft deferment in 1942—as did DiMag. Perhaps it was that the Yankee Clipper avoided controversy and Williams seemed to go looking for it that DiMaggio was able to get away with doing things that the Boston slugger was criticized for.

In the first game of the 1942 season, Williams was booed at FP because of his draft deferment headlines. He answered back with a three-run homer his first time at bat. The draft-deferred DiMaggio drew cheers at the Stadium.

A letter written to (and printed by) a Boston newspaper typified the controversy that swirled around Williams.

Ted Williams is the all-time, all-American adolescent. He never wears a necktie unless he wears it to bed. He'll never tip his cap to the guys who pay his over-stuffed salary. He'll never bunt, steal, hustle or take a sign . . . unless it suits his royal convenience. In short, he'll continue to be just what he has always been—the prize heel that ever wore a Boston uniform."

In 1942 the Red Sox were once again beaten out for the

American League pennant by the New York Yankees. Boston finished second to New York and Williams was runnerup (270–249) in the voting to a Yankee for the Most Valuable Player award. The moody slugger won the Triple Crown with a .365 batting average, 137 RBIs and 36 home runs, but Joe Gordon won the MVP award. Williams had eclipsed the Yankee infielder in every offensive category—including that of press relations. There were many who said that was the reason he lost out to Gordon. Ted's troubles with the draft board also contributed to negative feelings about him.

But even the Sox fans who booed and criticized Williams were incensed at the MVP balloting, especially since the award went to a Yankee. In 1941, Williams maintained that DiMaggio deserved the MVP award. Now the Boston outfielder was livid. He took out his feelings on the press; many reporters remembered and they worked their typewriters with a fury to get back at him.

"If his ego swells another inch, Master Ted Williams will not be able to get his hat on with a shoe horn," wrote Jack Miley in the *New York Post*. "When it comes to arrogant and ungrateful athletes, this one leads the league."

Criticism ticked Williams off. Fans cursed him. He cursed back. "Damn New England buzzards," was his expression for those who attacked him. When words failed him, he sometimes answered back with obscene gestures, stoking more controversy.

Throughout his career, Williams baiters used to line up in the left-field grandstand at Fenway where the corner runs close to the playing field. Fans armed with containers of beer would dare the Thumper to chase a fly ball within their pouring range. To protect Williams, the Boston management withheld selling seats in that area until all other grandstand seats were sold out.

They called him the Kid, and he acted like one. He fired a shiny new pistol from the box seats behind home plate at the left field scoreboard at FP and shattered some $400 worth of light bulbs. On another occasion, his fondness for firing a weapon shoved him into a new controversy.

There were many pigeons at Fenway Park. It was reported that each time the population became too large, the groundskeeper would shoot them. One day Williams went out with his 20-gauge shot gun and destroyed about 40 pigeons. Owner Tom Yawkey came out and joined Williams in the pigeon shoot. "By the time we were done," Williams said, "we knocked off seventy or eighty pigeons. We had a hell of a time." Reporters tipped off the humane society. And that was the end of Williams' pigeon shooting at Fenway. It was not the end of his running feud with the press.

Approached by a reporter who had attacked him, Williams lashed out, "You write crap stuff about me, and you want to get an interview. Get the hell away from me."

Two of Ted's severest critics were Boston writers. "No grown man in full possession of his faculties would make the vile gestures that Williams made," wrote Dave Egan in the *Boston Record.* And Harold Kaese snapped in the *Boston Globe* that "Ted Williams should do himself a favor. He should quit baseball before baseball quits on him."

Theodore Samuel Williams was many things, but he was not a quitter. In 1946 he recorded 38 home runs, batted .342, and led the league in runs scored, walks and slugging average. The Red Sox won the pennant and Williams won his first MVP award. It was a season in which he let his bat do his talking.

A winter operation had severely handicapped Joe Di-Maggio, and in 1947 he was able to engage in very little spring training. Driven to make up for lost time, he spent many hours taking extra batting practice. Asked by the Yankee management to pose for some Army recruiting posters, Joe Dee refused. He claimed he could not spare the time. He was fined $100—the first and only fine of his career. "What are you trying to do, Joe," Williams was supposed to have said, "steal my act?"

Before a Yankee-Sox game at the Stadium there was a home-run hitting contest. Williams easily won the contest for southpaws, powering deep drives into the right-field seats. No winner was announced for the right-handed batters. In the actual game, Joe Dee, unable to do anything in the pregame contest, slugged a three-run homer into the stands. When it mattered, DiMag was there.

Fans of Boston and New York passionately debated the relative merits of the Thumper and the Yankee Clipper. Others too joined in the banter and helped the rivalry along.

Joe Page, Yankee relief pitcher and DiMaggio's roommate, embittered with Joe McCarthy, his former Yankee manager, who had publicly criticized him for engaging in late-night drinking forays, was as much anti-Williams as he was pro-DiMaggio. Page delighted in putting a little extra on his fastball when he faced Ted. In Page's view, "Williams couldn't hold a candle to DiMag as a ball player."

Another who was part of the legion of loyalists for Di-Maggio was sportswriter Jimmy Cannon. "There was nothing they could teach Joe D. When he came to the big leagues it was all there. Other guys hit for higher averages, struck more home runs. But this is the whole ballplayer, complete and great. There are no defects to discuss."

In 1951, DiMaggio retired at the age of 36. The Yankee management attempted to coax him into performing in pinstripes for one more season, but he had too much pride and too much pain and too many defects. "He can't stop quickly," a scouting report prepared by the Dodgers for the 1951 World Series and published in *Life* magazine, said. "He can't throw real hard. You can take an extra base on him if he's in motion away from the line of the throw. He won't throw on questionable plays. He can't run and he can't pull the ball at all."

Joseph Paul DiMaggio left behind the memory of a man who moved about in the vast center field of Yankee Stadium with an almost poetical grace. He had played when he was fatigued, when he was hurt, when it mattered a great deal, and when it didn't matter at all. DiMag recorded a career average of .325, 361 home runs, eight World Series home runs, two batting championships. "Those statistics don't even tell the story," says DiMaggio's former teammate, pitcher Eddie Lopat. "What he meant to the Yankees, you'll never find in the statistics. He was the real leader of that club. DiMag was the best."

Even Ted Williams agreed. "I learned from DiMag," said the Sox slugger. "I was able to see that you could get on edge on the toughest pitcher by waiting on the pitch. Joe was one of the few hitters around who waited so long he seemed to hit the ball right out of the catcher's mitt. He was the best right-handed pull hitter I ever saw. DiMaggio was the greatest."

The Thumper singles out the Yankee Clipper as the greatest player he ever saw, but there are many who point Ted out as the greatest hitter. "Anytime anyone mentions the Boston Red Sox," says Mickey Mantle, who was signed for a $1,150 bonus in the back seat of a 1947 Oldsmobile, "the first thing that comes to my mind is Ted Williams. I don't think he was the greatest all-around player, but he could hit. I do think he was the greatest hitter that ever lived." In 1951, Mantle replaced DiMaggio as the Yankee superstar, just as the Yankee Clipper succeeded Babe Ruth.

With Joe DiMaggio gone, Ted Williams played on "with the best combination of power and average," in batting coach Charlie Lau's phrase, "that I ever saw. He more or less used half the field to hit in."

In 1956, Williams battled Mickey Mantle for the batting crown, just as he had in earlier years gone head-to-head with Joe Dee. Closing out the season against the Red Sox, Yankee pitchers held Williams to two hits in 11 attempts. Mantle managed six hits in nine at bats against Boston hurlers. Mantle wound up with a .353 average; Williams batted .345.

In 1957, Williams batted .388, his highest batting average since 1941. He was just five hits away from a .400 average. He was 39 years old, the oldest player in baseball history to win a batting title. The Yankees won the pennant. Mantle won the MVP award. All over New England a roar of disapproval was loosed. Tom Yawkey was livid. "The voting was done by some incompetent and preju-

Ted Williams (right) with two of his Yankee rivals:
Mickey Mantle (center) and Joe DiMaggio

diced people," he charged. Indeed, two Chicago writers voted Williams ninth and tenth in the MVP balloting.

In 1958, Williams again heard the boo-birds. After taking a called strike three in a game at the Fens, he threw his bat in rage and disgust at the umpire's decision. It hit Joe Cronin's housekeeper, who was sitting 70 feet away from home plate in the stands. On her way out of the park, headed to the hospital, the housekeeper asked, "Why are they booing Ted?" They cheered him, too, when he won his sixth batting title that season. He was 40 years old.

On September 28, 1960, at Fenway Park, before 10,454

fans, Ted Williams engaged in his last hurrah. There was a weekend series still to be played against the Yankees, but for Williams, this was the final game.

In the pregame ceremonies, Williams was given a silver bowl, a $4,000 check made out to the Jimmy Fund he had supported through all the years, and a standing ovation.

"If I were asked where I would have liked to have played," he said, his voice barely carrying over the crowd's roar, "I would have to say Boston . . . the greatest town in baseball and the greatest fans in America, despite the many disagreeable things said about me by the knights of the keyboard."

Then in his last major league at-bat, Williams slammed home run number 521 into the bullpen in right-center field. Those who might have booed him in the past stood and cheered as he circled the bases at the Back Bay ballyard for the last time, trotting into history. He crossed home plate, and he didn't tip his cap.

Theodore Samuel Williams had made his point. He had said at the start that he had wanted to be remembered as the greatest hitter who ever lived. And there were few who would have argued that he wasn't—even Joe DiMaggio, even the most rabid Yankee fan.

He ranks among the all-time leaders in home runs, runs batted in, total bases, slugging and batting average—all this despite having lost the equivalent of six seasons to injuries and military service. He was walked intentionally 33 times, an all-time season record. He averaged almost a walk a game: one out of every 4.5 at bats was a walk. His base-reaching percentage is the highest in baseball history. His 2019 walks place him second on the all-time list; eight times he led the American League in walks. He did it his way. And at age 42, in his fourth major league decade, he batted .310—34 points below his lifetime average.

DiMag was the Yankees and Williams was the Red Sox.

GREAT MOMENTS

Through 1981, there have been 1,611 games played between the Yankees and Red Sox. Virtually half the games have been played at little Fenway Park and the other half have played out in the big park, Yankee Stadium. Through the years, some of the greatest and most exciting moments in baseball history have held center stage in these games, inning by inning.

The intensity of the rivalry, with the added element of rabid fans and proud players, has added to the significance of these great moments.

Images remain—of Ruth and Gehrig, of Williams and

Doerr, of Pesky and Yaz and Fisk, of Rizzuto and Mapes and Larsen, of Cronin, of Foxx, of York. . . .

BABE RUTH'S FIRST HOME RUN—*May 6, 1915*

In the third inning at the Polo Grounds, twenty-year-old Babe Ruth slammed the first pitch off Yankee right-hander Jack Warhop into the second tier of the right-field grandstand for a home run. The first home run for Ruth came in his 18th time at bat in the major leagues.

As Ruth trotted around the bases running out the home run he had blasted off Warhop's underhand teaser, the 8,000 in attendance, including Red Sox owner Joseph Lannin, American League president Ban Johnson and sportswriters Damon Runyon and Heywood Broun, cheered him on. Runyan wrote, in his account of the game:

Fanning this Ruth is not as easy as the name and the occupation might indicate. In the third inning Ruth knocked the slant out of one of Jack Warhop's underhand subterfuges, and put the baseball in the right field stands for a home run. Ruth was discovered by Jack Dunn in a Baltimore school a year ago where he had not attained his left-handed majority, and was adopted and adapted by Jack for use of the Orioles. He is now quite a demon pitcher and demon hitter when he connects.

Ironically, the momentous first of Ruth's 714 career homers came against the team he would come to symbolize—the New York Yankees. The home run was his fifth major league hit. In ten times at bat in 1914 and eight times at the plate in 1915, he had notched three doubles and a single.

"Mr. Warhop of the Yankees," wrote Wilmot Giffin in the *New York Evening Journal,* "looked reproachfully at the opposing pitcher who was so unclubby as to do a thing like that to one of his own trade. But Ruthless Ruth seemed to think that all was fair in the matter of fattening a batting average."

Ruth's shot notwithstanding, the Yankees were able to eke out a 4–3, thirteen-inning triumph over the Red Sox and taint the Babe with the loss.

THE RECORD-SETTING 45TH GAME OF JOE DIMAGGIO'S 56-GAME HITTING STREAK—*July 2, 1941*

On the first day of July 1941, Joe DiMaggio tied the 43-year-old record of Wee Willie Keeler by hitting safely in both games of a doubleheader against the Red Sox. The Yankee Clipper had rapped out at least one hit in 44 straight games.

On July 2 the Yankees again faced the Red Sox. Joe Dee was intent on getting a hit in his 45th straight game and setting a new major league record. Dom DiMaggio was stationed in center field for the Red Sox. Joe had invited him to dinner that evening at his home.

In his first at-bat against Boston pitcher Herber Newsome, the Yankee Clipper smashed a long drive that was caught by Stan Spence. Joe Dee swung a bit more forcefully his second time up and drove the ball to center field. Breaking at top speed as he heard the crack of his older brother's bat against the ball, Dom ran it down and made a dramatic catch to rob Joe of his bid for an extra-base hit. The two brothers rarely showed emotion on the baseball field, but looking at each other this time from inside their Yankee and Red Sox uniforms, they showed how they felt. "It was a great catch," Joe recalled. "It was one of the best Dom ever made. I was tempted at that moment to withdraw the dinner invitation for that evening."

In his third turn at bat, with two teammates on base, hungering for a hit, frustrated twice, Joe took no chances. He belted the ball into the seats for what would be one of the 30 home runs he would hit that momentous 1941 season. He had the record, and it had come against the Boston Red Sox.

The New York center fielder and the Boston center fielder dined that evening. "While Dom lapped up my steak and ate my spaghetti," Joe recalled, "he had the audacity to tell me: 'You know, Joe, I couldn't have gone another inch for that ball.' "

JOE DIMAGGIO'S GRAND FINALE AT FENWAY PARK—
October 3, 1948

There were 31,304 fans at Fenway, and in Joe DiMaggio's phrase, "They had come to see Yankee blood." Jack Kramer had pitched the Sox to a 5–1 victory over New York the day before, and on this final day of the season, the Indians led Boston by one game in the race for the American League pennant.

"We had nothing except satisfaction to play for," recalls DiMag. "You might say there must have been a letdown in our play. But there wasn't. . . . It is never fun to lose, and besides, the league standings did not convince us that there were two better teams in the league."

For the Yankees and DiMaggio all that was at stake was pride. For the Red Sox everything was at stake. A win coupled with a Cleveland loss would force a play-off. The DiMaggio family was in the stands rooting for Boston. Dom had a chance for the World Series. Joe and the Yankees did not. In the first inning, Joe Dee doubled for one Yankee run. The Sox scored five times in the third. The Fenway faithful screamed at the scoreboard news that after three innings Detroit was leading Cleveland, 5–0.

In the Yankee fifth, Dobson was faltering for the Sox. DiMag came to the plate. Hurt and hobbled with a charley horse in both legs, the Yankee Clipper looked at his teammates on the basepaths: Rizzuto, who had singled, and Bobby Brown, who had doubled. He slammed a Dobson pitch off the left-field wall to cut the Sox lead to 5–4.

In the ninth inning, DiMag recorded his fourth hit of the game, a single. Yankee manager Bucky Harris, realizing that the game was virtually out of reach with his team trailing, 10–5, and knowing the pain that DiMag was feeling, sent in Steve Souchock to run for Joe Dee.

"I turned and started for the dugout," recalls DiMag. "I guess I was limping pretty bad. Anyway that's what they told me later. I'll never forget that crowd. It was standing and roaring like one man. I tipped my cap but it didn't stop. I looked up at the stands at this ovation they were giving to a guy who had tried to beat them. They were still yelling when I disappeared into the dugout. They didn't stop for another three or four minutes."

NEW YORK (A)	Ab.	H.	P.	A.
Riz'uto, ss	5	1	0	3
H'nr'h, 1b	3	0	5	0
Brown, 3b	5	1	1	0
J. Dim., cf	5	4	2	1
d So'chock	0	0	0	0
Berra, rf	2	0	1	0
Lindell, lf	3	1	3	0
Ba'r, lf, rf	3	0	2	0
Silvera, c	3	2	6	0
a Keller	0	0	0	0
Houk, c	0	0	2	0
St'w's, 2b	2	1	2	0
b W.J'ns'n	1	0	0	0
Cros'ti, ss	0	0	0	0
P'terf'd, p	0	0	0	0
Raschi, p	2	1	0	0
Reyn'ds, p	0	0	0	0
c Collins	1	0	0	0
Page, p	0	0	0	0
Totals	35	11	24	4

BOSTON (A)	Ab.	H.	P.	A.
D.Dim., cf	4	3	3	0
Pesky, 3b	5	1	3	2
Wil'ms, lf	4	2	2	0
Ste'ns, ss	5	2	1	5
Doerr, 2b	5	2	3	1
Spence, rf	1	0	0	0
G'dm'n, 1b	4	3	10	2
Tebb'ts, c	5	1	3	1
Dobson, p	2	0	2	2
E.J'ns'n, p	1	0	0	0
Ferriss, p	2	1	0	0
Totals	38	15	27	13

a Walked for Silvera in 8th.

b Grounded out for Stirnweiss in 7th.

c Lined out for Reynolds in 8th.

d Ran for J.DI MAGGIO in 9th.

New York	110	020	100 — 5
Boston	005	004	10x — 10

R—Rizzuto, Henrich 2, Brown, Bauer, D. DiMaggio 2, Pesky, Williams, Stephens 2, Doerr 2, Spence, Ferriss. RBI—J. DIMAGGIO 3, Stirnweiss, Bauer, Williams 2, Doerr 2, D. DiMaggio, Goodman 2, Tebbetts, Stephens 2. E—None. 2B—J. DIMAGGIO 2, Brown, Doerr, Williams 2, Ferriss. HR—D. DiMaggio, Stephens. DP—Pesky and Goodman,

Stephens, Doerr and Goodman. SO—Porterfield 1, Raschi 3, Reynolds 2, E. Johnson 1. BB—Porterfield 3, Raschi 2, Reynolds 1, Page 1, Dobson 3, E. Johnson 1, Ferriss 1. HO—Porterfield 6 in 2⅓, Raschi 5 in 3, Reynolds 3 in 1⅔. Dobson 6 in 4, E. Johnson 4 in 2, Ferriss 1 in 3, Page 1 in 1. Winner—E. Johnson. Loser—Porterfield. U—Rommel, Hubbard, McGowan and Passarella. A—31,304.

Cleveland lost that day and the Red Sox won, and the first play-off in American League history was the result—but the biggest winner was Joltin' Joe. On two bum legs he had racked out two doubles and two singles and driven in three runs.

After the game the DiMaggio brothers had a reunion. "Well," said Joe, "I hope you beat Cleveland tomorrow, Dom. I guess you felt like strangling me when I hit that shot off the wall in the fifth. I'm sure our family did."

"No, no," smiled Dom. "Don't ever tell Joe McCarthy [the Sox manager], but when you did it, I felt like applauding—everybody did."

THE JOE DIMAGGIO SHOW AT FENWAY PARK—
June 28–30, 1949

One of the most supercharged confrontations in all the years of the Yankee–Red Sox rivalry took place at Fenway Park on June 28–30, 1949. Joe DiMaggio called those three days in Boston "the most satisfying days of my life."

The Yankees were in first place, but the Sox were closing fast. Winners of ten of their last 11 games—the last four in a row—the Red Sox were confident as they prepared for a three-game series with the Bronx Bombers.

Relations between the two rivals was especially acrimonious. Yankee general manager George Weiss had publicly criticized player trades and purchases made by Boston with the St. Louis Browns, in which the Sox had picked up Ellis Kinder, Vern Stephens and others. "It's getting so that Boston is using the Browns as a farm team," said Weiss. "It's bad for baseball and bad for the American League."

There were 36,228 people crammed into Fenway for the Friday-night series opener. DiMaggio had missed the first 65 games of the season. He wore an orthopedic shoe elevated at the heel to relieve some of the pressure from bone chips that lingered from a winter operation on the right heel for a bone spur injury.

"The Boston thing was funny," recalled Joe Dee. "I got to play a little joke on Stengel. I flew up to Boston and went right to the ballpark. I put on my uniform and went out on the bench. The teams were on the field and Stengel had his back to me and was talking to reporters. He hadn't put out the starting lineup and they were asking him about it. I couldn't hear a word he was saying. I didn't say a word. He kept turning around and looking at me. I kept tying my laces. Finally, I gave him a nod and then he said to them in a loud voice, 'Now I can give you the lineup.' "

DiMaggio faced Boston pitcher McDermott. It was the Yankee Clipper's first American League at-bat in eight months. "McDermott," recalled DiMag, "could throw hard. My timing was off. I kept fouling pitch after pitch off to right field, but each time I kept hitting the ball closer to fair territory. Then I lined a hit over the shortstop's head. It felt real good."

His second time up, with Rizzuto on base, DiMag pounded a home run over the left-field wall. The partisan Boston crowd gave the Yankee center fielder a standing ovation as he trotted out the home run. "I don't think I was ever booed at Fenway," said DiMag. "The fans there always respected clean competition and good baseball."

The first game was frenzied competition and frenetic baseball. There was almost an altercation between Rizzuto and Johnny Pesky when the Sox infielder jammed his knee into the Scooter's face attempting to take Rizzuto out and break up a double play. In the eighth inning DiMag walked . A grounder was hit to the infield, and the Yankee Clipper darted toward second base, where Vern Stephens prepared to take the force-out throw. DiMag threw himself into Stephens. DiMag may not have remembered, but the thousands of Sox partisans booed. They booed him because they were furious at his intimidating move against Stephens. For the Sox, a message had been sent by the leader of the Yanks. He would tolerate no mayhem against any one of his teammates.

The game moved to the bottom of the ninth inning. The Yanks clung to a 5–4 lead. Joe Page was pitching. Ted Williams was batting. The tying run was on third base. There were two outs. Williams swung, bidding for an extra-base hit, but DiMag loped back into deep center field, gracefully catching the ball for the game's final out. The victory ended the Sox four-game winning streak.

The Yankees trailed in the second game, 7–1, after four innings, but no one in the crowded park thought the game was settled. They were right. Joe Dee slugged a three-run homer off Ellis Kinder to bring the Yanks close. In the seventh inning a Gene Woodling bases-loaded double tied the score. In the eighth inning, with Earl Johnson pitching for Boston and one Yankee on base, DiMag slugged the ball over the Green Monster and over the screen to give New York a 9–7, come-from-behind victory. Stoically, he ran out the home run as his Yankee teammates jumped to their feet in unison, with many partisan Boston fans. Someone held up a sign: "You can hate the Yankees, but you've got to love Joe Di-Maggio!"

Joe Page closed out the Sox in the ninth inning, and the Yanks once again added to the anti–New York consciousness-raising that was felt throughout New England.

Fenway Park was again virtually SRO as the third game was set to begin. A small plane circled above the little ballpark and trailing after the plane was a banner that proclaimed, "The Great DiMaggio."

Boston's Mel Parnell faced New York's Vic Raschi, and after seven innings the Yanks clung to a slim 3–2 lead. Then, with George Sternweiss and Tommy Henrich on base, DiMag smashed a three-run homer off the light tower. The Yanks won the game, 6–3.

In the three-game series, DiMag batted .455, recorded nine RBIs and slugged four home runs and one single. Even the most rabidly anti–Yankee fan and pro–Red Sox rooter was forced to admit that the "Joe DiMaggio Show" that played at Fenway Park June 28–30, 1949, would be remembered as one of the greatest sequences in baseball's greatest rivalry.

"I think," explained a delighted DiMaggio, "that I was the most surprised guy in the whole ballpark, the most surprised guy in all of Boston."

THE FINAL WEEKEND OF THE 1949 SEASON

The Red Sox had won 59 of their last 78 games and came into Yankee Stadium on October 1, 1949, for the final two games of the season needing just one victory to clinch the pennant. It was Joe DiMaggio Day. The 34-year-old DiMaggio, 18 pounds underweight, had come back after a serious bout with viral pneumonia to be honored on this last weekend of the season. His mother, Mrs. Rosalie DiMaggio, a gray-haired, stooped woman dying of cancer, had been flown in from California for the occasion. More than 140,000 would attend the two games and thousands more would tarry on the sidewalks listening to the play-by-play on the bulky, static prone portable radios.

A reporter asked Mrs. DiMaggio to name the best center fielder in baseball. "It's one of the two on the field today," she said. Yankee fans might have argued with a mother's prejudice, but fielding statistics for Joe and Dom reveal how closely matched they were. Joe played in 1,736 games in 13 years and recorded a .978 fielding average. Dom played in 1,399 games in ten years and recorded an identical .978 fielding average.

"If we don't win the pennant," the Yankee Clipper smiled, "it's nice to know my old manager Joe McCarthy and my brother Dom will win it."

The DiMaggio family occupied a box seat behind the Yankee dugout. Mel Allen presided as master of ceremonies. "I thank the good Lord for making me a Yankee," said DiMaggio, with tears streaming down his face. He later noted that it was only the second time in his

The brothers DiMaggio, Joe on the left and Dom on the right, flanking Ted Williams—a dream outfield

adult life that he had cried—the first time was in 1939, when Lou Gehrig exited as a Yankee.

"I could not help thinking of my teammates," Joe Dee said. "They had stood up all season despite 70-odd injuries. I knew every man was certain that the Red Sox were not going to 'steal' a prize from us at the very end, and I knew every man was waiting impatiently for the game to begin ... they must have thought: 'C'mon give the guy his presents and get on with the game. There is a pennant to be won.' "

Mel Parnell started the game for the Sox. A week before, he had defeated the Yankees for his 25th victory. Allie Reynolds was the Yankee starter. The Sox jumped all over Reynolds and piled up a 4–0 lead. Stengel yanked the "Super Chief" and brought in Joe Page. "Just hold them, Joe," barked Stengel. "Just hold them."

"We were behind 4–0," recalls Rizzuto who was initially scouted by Boston and placed on hold while they deliberated about another shortstop prospect. Rizzuto did not wait for the Sox to get back to him. He signed with the Yanks. The other shortstop signed with the Red Sox, but he was sold to the Brooklyn Dodgers without having ever played a game for Boston. His name was Pee Wee Reese. "We were behind but not beaten," continues Rizzuto. "I went up to hit and Boston catcher Birdie Tebbets started to talk to me. That was not unusual. Birdie would always talk a lot to me or spit on my shoe or kid around like that. But this time he got me angry. 'Oh, Phil, we're gonna be drinkin' a lot of champagne tonight and we're gonna have a party because we're gonna clinch the pennant today and a kid from the minors will be pitching for us tomorrow.' Holy Cow, I was annoyed. I told Casey and some of the other guys when I got back to the bench and they were not too happy with what Birdie had said. I don't think that was the only factor in getting us back in the game, but it sure helped."

Joe Dee's ground-rule double started the Yankee comeback. And the Bronx Bombers pulled the game out on an eighth-inning home run by Johnny Lindell that provided the margin of victory in a 5–4 Yankee win. It was only the sixth homer of the season for Lindell, a .229 hitter. Perhaps it was the needling of Tebbets, the presence of DiMag or the sight of the Red Sox uniforms—whatever, the season came down to the final game on October 2 with Boston and New York tied for first place.

Caught in the middle between the dejected Boston fans and the jubilant Yankee rooters was Mrs. Rosalie Di-Maggio. She was seated on a chair under the stands for security purposes when she was told by a guard, "Joe will be awhile. Would you like to go to a place where you will be more comfortable?"

"Please," she replied, "take me over to Dominick. He lose today."

On Sunday, the line for bleacher seats was more than a block long. Vic Raschi opposed Ellis Kinder, a 20-game winner. DiMaggio, Berra and Henrich played together for just the 15th time that season of patching and pruning of an injury-ridden Yankee team.

A Rizzuto triple and an infield out produced the first Yankee run, and that was the only scoring as the shadows of autumn fell over the "House That Ruth Built" and the game moved to the top of the eighth. Ellis Kinder had allowed just two hits. In one of those moves that would infuriate Sox fans for years and be the subject of thousands of arguments on street corners and bars, McCarthy, scrounging for runs, pinch-hit for Kinder. The Sox could not capitalize. The score was still 1–0 New York as Parnell came in to pitch the bottom of the eighth inning.

The Yankees scored four times, and thousands screamed out their joy. In the top of the ninth, Boston fought back. They scored three times—two of the runs coming in on a triple over DiMag's head slugged by Bobby Doerr. The Yankee Clipper was exhausted and removed himself from the game. The Yankees won, 5–3, for the first of Stengel's five straight pennants.

DiMaggio said later, "This team was the gamest, fightin'est bunch of guys that ever lived." Stengel, seized with victory, screamed out in the locker room, "Fellas, I want to thank you all for going to all the trouble to do this for me."

And in the visitors' dressing room, a dejected Kinder moaned. "If the old man woulda let me stay in, we woulda won the game."

The fans of the Yankees turned their attention to the World Series. The fans of the Red Sox licked their wounds and prepared to play back through another long winter the frustration of being bridesmaids for the second straight year.

CONTRASTS—*September 24, 1950*

The sad memory of the Sox squandering away the pennant on the last day of the seasons of 1948 and 1949 hung over Boston like a cloud. "Losing those pennants hurt," notes Johnny Pesky. "There can be no doubt about that. We had a great club in those years, and we should have won at least three pennants. But if the Yankees beat us in some that hurt, we beat them in some that hurt, too."

With ten games to go in the 1950 season, the Yankees and Tigers were tied for first place. On September 24, Boston came into the Stadium. Managed by Steve O'Neil, who had replaced Joe McCarthy, the Sox trailed Detroit and New York by just two games. "It was a real opportunity for us," recalls Pesky.

There were 63,998 in attendance; many of them had come in from New England to keep the faith with the Sox. Eddie Lopat's junkballs broke the backs of the Boston sluggers as the Yanks pounded out an 8–0 win. Joe Dee chipped in with a two-run homer. The Yankee win coupled with a Detroit loss seemed to make all of New York sense the kill—another Yankee pennant. More than 66,000 jammed Yankee Stadium for the second game with the Sox, who got on the scoreboard first, via a Ted Williams home run. It was a day of scoreboard watching, and the Yankees cheered along with their fans when the news that Detroit had lost again to the Indians was posted. The big money game spurred the Yanks on. Berra slashed four hits, one a triple; Rizzuto recorded three hits, one a home run. And the Yanks nailed down a 9–5 win over the Sox. It was Casey Stengel's second straight pennant.

Critics and disgusted Sox fans claimed that the team from Boston lacked the leadership and the "take-charge" mentality of the Yankees. Eddie Lopat, who paced the Yankees five years in a row in ERA, wore his pinstripes with pride, and while he doesn't comment on the Sox, his insights into what made the Yankees what they were provides an interesting perspective on the makeup of the two teams.

"We played a doubleheader in Washington," notes Lopat. "We won the first game; the second game ended after ten innings in a 3–3 tie. Yogi [Berra] didn't catch the second game. Charlie Silvera caught. He came up three times with the bases loaded and made an out three times. You know Yogi—three times up with the bases full and something would've popped. After the second game was called, DiMag was in the clubhouse about to fall down, he was so exhausted from the heat and the strain of playing both games. Yogi was jumping around. 'What in the world are you so happy about?' DiMag asked Yogi. 'We didn't do so bad today,' Yogi said. 'You're twenty-one years old and you can't catch a doubleheader,' DiMag lit into him. You could hear a pin drop. Then two and three other fellows lit into Yog as well. The next few years Yogi caught 152–153 games a season. He was afraid to ask Stengel to get out. He knew he'd ask him, 'What's the story?' That was part of the Yankee story, the Yankee way—call it leadership if you want."

Williams was a great admirer of Casey Stengel's. "He was a great manager and had a great sense of character," said the former Red Sox slugger. "He is right up there with Judge Landis, Ty Cobb and Babe Ruth when it comes to baseball greatness. He was the real leadership— not the players. When guys like McDougald or Coleman decided to take charge and calm down a pitcher, it was because Casey probably picked his nose or rubbed his ear telling them to get in there and slow down the pitcher to stall for time to give another guy a chance to warm up."

Casey was a part of the rivalry and apart from the rivalry. He was a special character, a special person. Hired as Yankee manager on October 12, 1948, just two months after Babe Ruth died at age 53, Stengel seemingly was an odd choice. "We thought we got us a clown," recalls Lopat. "We just sat back and watched him. It was a treat for him to be with us after all the donkey clubs he had been with. Casey was something. He could make the moves. He was pure baseball."

ALLIE REYNOLDS' SECOND NO-HITTER—
September 28, 1951

The Red Sox and Yankees had each played 150 games in the 1951 American League season. Surging, charging, the Yankees played host to Boston at Yankee Stadium before nearly 40,000 fans, needing just two wins to wrap up their third straight pennant, one win to clinch a tie.

Allie Reynolds was tabbed by Casey Stengel to face the powerful Red Sox lineup. Inning after inning, the fast-balling Yankee right-hander showed his mastery over Dom DiMaggio, Johnny Pesky, Ted Williams, Clyde Volmer, Billy Goodman, Lou Boudreau, Freddy Hatfield, and Aaron Robinson. The Yanks scored two runs in the first inning off stylish Mel Parnell, two more in the bottom of the third, another run in the fourth inning and added two more in the sixth to make the score 7–0. A Gene Woodling home run made the score 8–0 as Reynolds took the mound for the top of the ninth inning. Not only had Yankee batters humiliated the Boston pitching staff, but the Super Chief had also humbled the potent Boston lineup. He had not allowed a hit, and inning after inning he had gotten stronger in his bid for his second no-hitter of the season.

Pinch hitter Charlie Maxwell led off for the Sox and fouled out. He just could not get around on the fast stuff Reynolds was firing up. Dom DiMaggio wiped his glasses, kicked a bit at the dirt and stepped in to the batter's box. Joe's brother was patient while Reynolds was impatient. Attempting to overpower the Sox center fielder, Allie put too much on his pitches and walked Dom. The third batter of the inning was the combative

Johnny Pesky. Reynolds fanned him. It was the Yankee star's ninth strikeout of the day.

Ted Williams moved out of the on-deck circle and slowly took his position in the batter's box. He was all that stood between Reynolds and the no-hitter, between the Yankees and their clinching of their third straight pennant. Winding up his tenth straight .300 season, the gangly Williams looked disdainfully out at Reynolds on the pitcher's mound. It was a classic match up: power right-handed pitcher versus scientific left-handed slugger.

As Reynolds looked in to catcher Yogi Berra for the sign and checked DiMaggio at first base, he heard the screams of fans: "Walk him. Walk him. Don't pitch to that guy."

Later Reynolds admitted, "I was very much aware of the no-hitter and the ninth inning and all I had to get out was Williams. Most times I tried to walk that damn guy. I just couldn't pitch to him. In my opinion, it was just stupid to let an outstanding hitter like him beat you. I walked a lot of people, but it was smart to walk Williams."

On this day, Reynolds had made up his mind he would pitch to Williams. The first pitch was a fastball—strike one. The second pitch was again a fastball. Williams uncoiled at it and fouled the ball in the air behind home plate. Berra circled about under the ball and was poised to catch it when at the last moment it darted off the edge of his glove. Reynolds and Berra collided. The laboring pitcher helped Yogi to his feet. "Don't worry, Yog, we'll get him next time."

Berra, who recalls "that Williams was the greatest hitter I ever had to catch against—he used to take pitches I would swing against," returned to take up his catcher's position.

"You blew it," snarled Williams. "You son of a bitches put me in a hell of a spot. Now I've got to bear down even harder even though your man has a no-hitter going."

The Boston slugger choked up ever so slightly on his bat. He peered out at Reynolds. "I called for the same pitch, the same fastball," recalls Berra. Williams swung. The pitch was fouled off near the Yankee dugout. Berra raced back. "Lotsa room, Yogi, lotsa room," screamed Tommy Henrich. "You can get it." Yogi got it.

Yankee fans were jubilant. Red Sox fans were dejected. "I just missed the first one and caught the second one," Yogi said calmly. Reynolds had posted his second no-hitter in the 1951 season, and the Yankees had clinched their third consecutive pennant.

A postscript to that memorable pennant-clinching performance is recalled by Bill Crowley, who broadcast the action as a Yankee announcer. "That winter I was in Toots Shor's in New York. A woman came over to me and told me that she listened to the game and was keeping score for her son while he was away at school. At the same time she was hosting her bridge club with her best china dishes. 'When you yelled out that Yogi dropped the ball, I got so excited that I dropped the dishes. Bill Crowley, you owe me a set of dishes for scaring me like that.' "

ROGER MARIS'S 61ST HOME RUN—*October 1, 1961*

The New York Yankees and the Boston Red Sox met in the final three games of the 1961 season at Yankee Stadium. Amidst the trappings of the greatest rivalry in baseball, Roger Maris was questing after baseball's most famous record—home run number 61, the one that would break Babe Ruth's single-season mark.

Throughout the season the Yankee outfielder had been badgered, bothered, besieged with the same question: "Will you break the Babe's record?" Maris responded alternately with disdain, distance, anger and sometimes rage: "Don't ask me about the fucking record anymore," he would shout. "I don't give a shit about the record. All I care about—all I'm interested in—is that we win the pennant."

Red Sox pitchers took the field affirming a desire not to surrender home run number 61 and allow Maris to break the Ruth record that had stood for 34 seasons. The three games were played out in an atmosphere of controversy. Commissioner Ford Frick had ruled that if Maris hit number 61, it would be inscribed in the record book with an asterisk to indicate that Ruth had recorded 60 in a 154-game season whereas Maris had played in a season of 162 games.

The Frick ruling angered Yankee fans, who carried placards that announced: "Frick—Up Your Asterisk!" Maris was mellower. "Commissioner Frick makes the rules," he said. "If all I am entitled to will be an asterisk, it will be all right with me."

Don Schwall of Boston stopped Maris in the first game of the series. Bill Monbouquette of Boston stopped Maris in the second game of the series. It came down to the final game of the season: Roger Maris of the New York Yankees against Tracy Stallard, a 24-year-old Boston right-hander.

Stallard retired Maris in his first at-bat. In the fourth inning, Maris made contact with a 2–0 Stallard pitch. He smashed the ball into the lower right-field deck, 360 feet from home plate. The historic shot brought the 23,154 in the stands to their feet. Maris trotted out the home run into the history books, relieved and happy, the normal tight and taciturn look on his face, gone. A youngster jumped out on to the field. He grabbed Maris's hand as the slugger passed first base. Maris shook hands. He shook hands with Yankee coach Frank Crosetti and rounded third heading for home. In front of the Yankee dugout, his teammates formed a human wall and would not allow Maris to enter. Four times he tried to find refuge in the dugout and each time he was pushed out onto the playing field. Finally, the reticent Maris waved his cap to the screaming, jubilant audience to history at the stadium. And then the human wall dissolved and Maris was allowed to enter the relative sanctuary of the dugout.

It was the only hit Maris was able to manage that day, and the only run scored as the Yankees nipped Boston, 1–0. "If I never hit another home run," Maris said later, "this is the one they can never take away from me."

THE YANKEE MASSACRE AT BOSTON—*June 17–19, 1977*

It was a windy weekend at Fenway Park and the 103,910 fans who came to watch the Yankees battle the Red Sox for the lead in the American League East got their share of thrills—especially if they were Sox fans.

The Sox humiliated the Yankees, 9–4, 10–4 and 11–1. In

the first game Catfish Hunter was shelled for four homers in the first inning. And before the thousands of gleeful Fenway Park partisans and a national TV audience, Yankee manager Billy Martin yanked Reggie Jackson out of the Saturday game. Martin claimed Jackson wasn't hustling. The two almost came to blows in the dugout as they screamed out their hostility to each other.

Martin was miffed that Jackson moved too slowly after a ball hit to right field and dispensed Paul Blair as Reggie's replacement. Jackson's exit was accentuated by loud booing throughout the park. "When they don't hustle, I don't accept that," Martin said later. "When a player shows the club up, I show the player up."

The Sox showed up the Yanks in that second game, pounding five homers. Yaz hit two; Bernie Carbo belted a pair and George Scott hit one.

The day of the final game the *Boston Herald American* headline read: "YANKS GO DOWN FIGHTING THEMSELVES." Denny Doyle homered for the Sox with two men on in the fourth inning to continue the Boston barrage on Yankee pitching. It was Doyle's first home run in 204 games. Carbo chipped in with another home run in the seventh inning.

In the final Red Sox plate appearances of the tumultuous series, Boston fans were screaming for more long-range hits. And they got them.

Jim Rice homered. Yaz followed with another homer. And George Scott, one out later, slammed another homer to cap the 11–1 runaway.

The "Yankee Massacre" set several league records: most home runs in three games (16), four games (18), five games (21). Yaz had slammed four home runs and driven in ten runs. Scott's home run hitting enabled him to take over the league lead in circuit clouts.

Some Yankee zealots claimed that Boston's rout was due to the strong wind that was blowing in Fenway that weekend, but Sox fans, elated at the sweep of the Yanks that gave Boston a 10–1 homestand record and the division lead, merely smiled. "The Yankees," a happy Sox fan said, "had the same wind blowing all weekend and they didn't hit one home run."

SEVEN-RUN EIGHTH-INNING RALLY BY SOX TOPS YANKS,
September 19, 1981

The Yanks and Sox met at Fenway Park before more than 32,000 fans on September 19, 1981. Ron Guidry opposed Mike Torrez. Boston sought to break the Yank's Fenway Park winning streak. Going into the game the Yankees had won nine straight in Boston's ball park.

Guidry coasted along allowing just one run in seven innings showing the form that enabled him to post an 8–2 career record against the Sox, and three wins in three starts at Fenway. Mike Torrez pitched according to pattern, too. The ex-Yankee, with just one win against his former teammates in 11 decisions, was pounded for eight hits and five runs in seven innings.

Yankee manager Bob Lemon asked Ron Guidry how he felt after the New York southpaw pitched the seventh inning. Winner of six of seven starts in the second half of the 1981 season, Guidry had not completed any of the starts and had not hurled more than seven innings in any of the games. "I said I felt all right," recalled Guidry. "I said I'd go ahead and start the next inning. Lemon said okay. Then when we had the long inning in the top of the eighth, I told him he might as well bring in someone right then. I could've gone out, but I might not have had anything. Why bring in someone with men on base when you can start an inning and not be in trouble?"

Guidry's exit and the entrance of Ron Davis in relief was when the Yankee trouble began. Davis got Jerry Remy on a ground ball to second. The tall Yankee reliever then struck out Dwight Evans.

There were two men out in the bottom of the eighth inning when Jim Rice came to bat. "With two out and nobody on base," recalled Carl Yastrzemski, who was waiting in the on-deck circle, "I didn't think we could do anything with one of the best relief pitchers in baseball facing us."

Rice singled. Yaz walked. A Carney Lansford single drove in the second Sox run. The faithful at Fenway were hysterical. Boston had momentum. What was happening was an instant replay of hundreds and hundreds of other Fenway late-inning rallies. It didn't matter to the screaming fans that only the night before, Davis had retired all seven batters he faced while preserving a 6–4 Yankee win over the Sox. This was another game.

Davis faced Dave Stapleton who managed to ground out a double down the right field line. Yaz scored with the third Sox run. And Lansford came in with the fourth Boston tally when Reggie Jackson muffed the ball in right field. A flustered Davis walked Tony Perez. With the score now 5–4 Yankees, Lemon replaced Davis with Dave LaRoche.

Joe Rudi lined a single to right off LaRoche. Stapleton scored to tie the game. Rick Miller worked a 3–0 count and then looked down at Eddie Yost, coaching at third base, expecting the "take" sign. "I saw nothing," Miller recalled, "and I was surprised. Then I said, 'Why should you be surprised? He wants you to get that extra swing.' "

The ex-Yankee Ralph Houk gambled. "It was a helluva gamble," smiled the Major. "I never expected what happened."

LaRoche recalls: "With a 3–0 count, I just threw a fast ball and attempted to get a strike."

It was a strike, and Miller sent the ball high and deep into Boston's bullpen in right centerfield for a home run. The shot capped the seven-run Sox eighth inning and their 8–5 victory.

FANFARE

Some are old; some are young. Some are just New York Yankee fans while others root strictly for the Sox. All of the fans are outspoken—especially those who have a special interest in *Baseball's Greatest Rivalry*. What follows is a sampling of some of that fanfare:

The Yankees are the rich man's team. They're snobs. Boston is human and not so good, but they can surprise you. I do not like George Steinbrenner. He's too haughty, too high and mighty. He represents what the Yankees have always been like. There's too much arrogance there.

I like the Red Sox because they remind me of an old time team. Their uniforms, their ballpark, is the way baseball was. The Sox are natural. The Yankees are plastic, a store bought team with a man who thinks he's a king who owns them. That's why I root for Boston and root against the Yankees even though I've lived almost all of my life in New York City.

Sam Bernstein, Brooklyn, N.Y.

I'm a Yankee fan. They're winners. The way the Red Sox play is like the repeated sailing of the Titanic.

Thor Hansen, New York City

One thing I could always count on was watching the Bronx Bombers on a Sunday afternoon. Pop and my brothers would tune in to hear the Scooter describe the action. Rizzuto would suffer along with each strike and give a sincere "Holy Cow" when the Yanks homered. Needless to say, so did my loyal Yankee family. Even though I have been brainwashed by Yankee pinstripes all my life, I admire the Boston Red Sox. Their attitude toward baseball is the way a team develops character. Boston's teams seem to play for the love of the sport; they have heart and great fans. Boston and New York fans are die-hard, hard on a player when he fails and right there to cheer when he succeeds.

Circo Tudisco, Brooklyn, N.Y.

I was a senior at Brown in the spring of 1963, when the Sox were somewhat interesting after years of poor teams. Yaz, Radatz, Monbo, as I recall, made the team a contender for a good part of the season. That was also the year of the police dog—Birmingham, Alabama, most notably, but even the Providence police used their dogs against Brown students who walked downtown the wrong way through the bus tunnel one May evening on a lark. Not to be outdone, the Boston police cleared the bleachers one night of a Yankee game with its K-9 corps. Several of my college chums and I had gone to the game, and were sitting close behind the Sox bullpen. We were drinking beer, to be sure, since you could and we did bring your own in those days. But we were shocked when some creeps in the center-field section began throwing empty cans at Mickey Mantle. As the game progressed, the cans became empty. They made what I have to admit was an entertaining sound and sight as they tumbled end-over-end, spewing foam and fizz en route to Mantle of the incredibly thick neck. I forgot exactly what intervening steps were taken, but in the final moments of the incident, I think we were standing on the field in the right-field corner, watching the Boston blue with dogs on leash, sweep back and forth, until no one was left in the bleachers. We scrambled over the fence into the right-field sections, and we watched the rest of the game, but not before we had shouted "Birmingham, Birmingham," at the cops. The event was born of several conflicting things: some genuine hatred of the Yankees and Mantle, some Fenway bleacherism and all the besotted and bestoned things it has always meant, and some puckish joy at the sound and sight of a flying beer can. . . .

Tom Generous, *Wallingford, Conn.*

I won't buy a pinstripe suit because of those damn Yankees.

137

Maybe it's because of my love affair with the Dodgers that my antagonism toward the Yankees has always been deeply felt. I lived in Brownsville and going to Ebbets Field was like going home to sit in an old, worn but oh-so-comfortable armchair. And watching a game there was like watching it in my own living room.

But were they kicked around. Although the Yanks never played the Brooks during the regular season, they were every Dodger fan's bitter enemy: smug, arrogant, and so talented. The Bronx Bombers versus the Brooklyn Bums.

Maybe it was because the Red Sox were only a shuttle-flight away that they became every Dodger fan's last great hope to knock down and out those pinstripers and re-claim the world for humility. The Red Sox. Now there was a class team: bright, brave, and human.

There was Williams. Then there was Yastrzemski. They played for a team that never lost its dignity on or off the field though hardly stopping the Yankees. And for me, there was Jimmy Piersall. What was he doing in Bos-ton? He should have been playing ringolevio with kids on Empire Boulevard before each home game in Brooklyn. And oh, would he have loved Happy Felton.

The Yankees were New York rich; the Red Sox were New England gritty. The Red Sox were my team in the American League because they weren't afraid to take on the Yankees. They were like an older brother fighting where you couldn't. Their day will come. And when it does, I'll be dancing on Empire Boulevard.

Alan A. Kay, *East Meadow, Long Island, N.Y.*

Reggie Jackson—"Mr. October"—who always seemed to be "up"
against the Sox any month

I remember those Yankee fans back at school, at Harvard. They were small, peculiar looking people with horn rimmed glasses who had never played any sport and had to identify with a superior force. They'd come in to the TV room at Lowell House and emit shreiks of glee whenever the Yankees scored. I expect though they all grew up someday to be advertising executives or always have to be right.

Anonymous

My grandfather always hated the Yankees. I picked it up. Reggie is not a real Yankee—he's a hotshot. He likes to come out here to Fenway and be booed and stuff. The one I hate the most is Bucky Dent because of that home run in 1978. The last few years the Sox always lose but that's part of being a Boston fan. They build you up and then they blow it in August or September so you lament all winter. If they won, you wouldn't know what to do all winter. I love Fenway. You can't beat this park, and you can't beat the bleacher seats although they keep raising the price. I have been to New York City but never to the Stadium. I wouldn't want to live in New York City. I dislike it there. If I ever went to the Stadium, I would never wear my Boston cap—it would probably be dangerous.

Will LaGace, *Cambridge, Mass.*

I was an eleven-year-old growing up in the South Bronx who cried when the Dodgers were pulled out by O'Malley to California. I asked my father is there any owner in baseball who looks at the sport the way I do. My father answered, "Tom Yawkey." And the Red Sox have been my team ever since.

Scott Russell, *New York City*

I have been a Yankee fan since 1932. Red Sox–Yankee games have always been fierce competition. I remember the fight between Jake Powell and Archie McKain in 1938. I remember in 1939 how the Red Sox led by their manager and shortstop Joe Cronin beat the Yanks five straight at the Stadium to cut the lead to a few percentage points. But the Yanks went on to win their 4th straight flag. Then there were the Williams' homers and later the Williams shift, with George Sternweiss, the second baseman on the Yankees, playing in short right field. But of all the games played, I will always remember Saturday October 1—Joe DiMaggio Day. Each fan was given a photo of Joe. I still have mine. Allie Reynolds started for the Yankees against Mel Parnell (who earlier made the statement that the bat boy could pitch tomorrow, the last game of the season). The Yankees won on October 1, and on October 2 they won again, and one of the pitchers used by the Red Sox was not the bat boy but Mel Parnell. I always thought about Joe McCarthy. He could have been only the second manager to win the pennant with three different teams. A playoff in 1948 and the final game of 1949 denied him the chance. There is a lot to remember and to talk about when one mentions the Yankee–Red Sox rivalry.

Walter C. Robertson, *Hempstead, Long Island, N.Y.*

My first game was at Yankee Stadium in 1938. I was eleven years old. It was the Memorial Day doubleheader. Jimmy Foxx and Lou Gehrig and those guys played. I've been coming to Yankee Stadium ever since. I've been a season-ticket holder since '66. I am involved in baseball chapels so I get involved in both teams. I don't go around telling everyone I'm a Yankee fan. Before games I meet with the Yankees in the locker room and the Red Sox and other teams in their locker rooms. It's hard to hate the Red Sox, but I get very upset at some of the Yankee fans getting bombed and acting disgracefully.

David Swanson, *New York City*

It's the best part of the season always when they play against each other. I go to about 20 games a year. I'm a real loyal Yankee fan. I have to admit the two teams play best when they play each other.

Rob Aldridge, *Jersey City, N.J.*

It's not the Boston fans that cause the problems, it's the Yankee fans. If Boston is behind, the Boston fans will root their players on. If the Yankees are behind, they'll look to pick a fight with the Boston fans. In the old days a lot of the fans would get drunk before they came to the game and let out their anxieties. You don't find that as much anymore. Now at the stadium there are pot smokers and more mellow types . . . you get an occasional fist fight over a play. . . .

Yankee Stadium Security Guard

I like wearing this "Yankees Suck" shirt. The white letters on the red shirt makes the message clear. I don't hate nobody. I love sports. To each his own. I come up to the Stadium through New England, Connecticut and up the Merritt Parkway and I'm here. I been a Red Sox fan for 35 years. I always stay overnight in Hackensack, New Jersey and I make my own good times. I'm a sport. And if I can't be a sport—I act like a sport. The worst thing that ever happened to me since I've been following baseball was when Bucky Dent hit that home run against us. It sunk me down all winter. I never thought he could reach that wall, but he did.

Lefty Laroche, *Boston, Mass.*

I'll always come to Yankee Stadium and wear this Boston cap. I'm a New Yorker but as a very young kid the first game I ever saw was at Fenway Park. I fell in love with the team, but each year they come up short. The front office stinks. I get beer thrown at me. I've had a couple of fights. I don't take the hat off. Someday the Red Sox will really come through.

Bill Maesfield, *Staten Island, N.Y.*

I'm a Yankee fan and I don't like the city of Boston because it's a very racist town. You've got Jim Rice on that team, but that is about it. Black people don't come around where the ballpark is. It's an Irish neighborhood and riots break out there. I know that for a fact. My brother lives in Boston, but I'm a native New Yorker. Knowing what I know about Boston, I would never go to Fenway Park.

Anonymous

I hate the Yankees and love the Sox. One of my friends got hit right in the mouth at the Stadium for wearing a Boston cap. I still wear mine. When I leave the stadium, I put it in my pocket. I made these earrings with the pictures of Red Sox on them in 1968. They were a product of my imagination. I'm afraid to wear the earrings to Yankee Stadium. I put them on after I'm in my seat. I live about 50 miles from Manhattan. I've never been to Fenway, but I'd love to be there one day to see a game. I love the Red Sox because of Ted Williams. He was my idol growing up, and I think he was the most marvelous person God ever put on the face of the earth when it comes to baseball. Ted made me a Red Sox fan. My name is Bo but not as in Derek.

Bo Field, *Kearney, N.J.*

I think we're getting a little raw. Some of those fellows walking about with buttons and tee shirts that say "Boston Sucks."

Herb Mencke, *Somerville, N.J.*

The great thing about moving from Rhode Island to Brookline Mass. was our new proximity to Fenway Park. It was nothing for my brother Bobby and I to get on the trolley and make the ten-minute ride to the ballpark. We see as many games as we can, especially when the Sox play the Yankees. Our grandfather has been a big Sox fan since he came to this country in the 1920s. He remembers everything, all the old stars, even when Babe Ruth played for Boston. So it's been kind of a family tradition rooting for the Red Sox. It's rooting for New England as opposed to New York.

Eric Portnoy, *Brookline, Mass.*

I came to America in the 1920s. Almost immediately I became interested in baseball, especially because of the Boston Red Sox. The team was not too good, but sitting in the bleachers in Fenway Park was a thrilling experience. I went with my friends, my sons, later on with my grandsons. In the beginning, I sat in the bleachers, but as the years moved on, I moved closer and closer to home plate. I'm in my eighties now, so most of the time I watch the games on TV, but I'm still a big Red Sox fan. Half my family settled in the Boston area, the rest in New York so there was always this rivalry over where we chose to live. The Yankees represented New York, a little too big, a little too proud. Boston is my kind of town. The Red Sox Are Boston.

Sam Skoler, *Quincy, Mass.*

I grew up in Boston and one of the reasons I have detested the Yankees so much is that they have beaten us with so much regularity. Every time the Yankees beat us here in Fenway, it's special frustration. The Dent home run was the worse moment. Today the average fan has not cemented relations with the Red Sox, possibly because of the fan and possibly because of the new Red Sox teams with all the changes. . . . It's not a Yawkey team— it's owned by a conglomerate. It's not that we are being entertained, it's that we feel we are being drained and that everything is the almighty dollar.

Anonymous, *Lynn, Mass.*

Every year I go to Yankee and Red Sox games at the Stadium and at Fenway. I wear my Boston cap. At the Stadium people always yell at me. They tell you to shove it and do this and do that with it. They say we are losers, that the Red Sox don't win. I'll always remember that lucky pop fly home run [by] Bucky Dent. I'll never forget it as long as I live, I won't. I cried all winter. It could have been Fred Stanley or somebody else. It was a cheap fluke

Primed for perfection: Phil Rizzuto, Joe DiMaggio, Yogi Berra and Jerry Coleman

thing. I grew up around here and the Yankees have always been so successful I can't understand why younger people go for them. I know it runs in the family but they have been standing for too much success for too long. I just like to see the little guy win. The Red Sox should win for a change. It burns me the way free agents all seem to want to play in the city of New York—why?

Gary Williams, *Bergenfield, N.J.*

I don't say I hate the Red Sox. I just have always been a Yankee fan. My father was a Yankee fan and it's more or less been a tradition. Yankee, Yankee, Yankee! I was

146

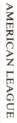

*Tom Yawkey—the man who took the Sox out of the wilderness
and made them Boston's pride*

seven years old before I knew there was another team. Mickey Mantle was my hero. He could play.

Jimmy Johnson, *Raleigh, N.C.*

I'm just wearing this Yankee cap to keep my head cool. I'm from Florida, just visiting at the Stadium. I figure the Yankees have had their day and it's time for another team to take over. They've won enough pennants and championships.

Hank Torcivia, *Miami Beach, Fla.*

I came up for the series. It's my first trip to the Stadium. I'm impressed by the Stadium but not the fans. I respect the Yankees, but I don't like them. I don't go for them no way. My loyalty goes back for the Red Sox to the Ted Williams era. We always rooted for the Sox.

Dan Letchworth, *Raleigh, N.C.*

I hate Steinbrenner. I liked Yawkey. When he died, it was like a curse. We beat up people who don't like the Red Sox. Boston fans are the worst. They love you when you're good and they hate you when you're bad. They hated Reggie because he went for the bucks and he's such a showboat. I love Fenway Park. These bleacher seats are special seats and the park is special too, with its little spots and crannies.

Ken Evans, *Cambridge, Mass.*

I like the Red Sox, but I hate the Yankees even more. The Yankee owner George Steinbrenner, or General as he's known, is wasting his time and money trying to grab up all the best players with his millions. They win a lot, but I don't think he gets his money's worth—look at what happened in the 1981 World Series. George has had about three or four managers in the last few years. Give these managers a break. How does he expect them to perform their managerial duties if he keeps telling them what to do—then if the team doesn't play the way he wants it to, he fires the manager. The Red Sox are calm—there's too much pressure in the Yankee organization that has nothing to do with baseball.

Astley Davy, *Bronx, N.Y.*

We've got a bit of a slew of Yankee fans right here in Boston and some of them come and wear Yankee caps and boo the Sox and first thing you know there are words and then a fist fight. Some of them get tanked up before they come in here and that helps the rowdyism. . . . The Yankees have had so many championships and we haven't and that has caused a lot of frustration. In '78, they should have never had a playoff. Zimmer left Hobson in too many times making errors and he knew he was hurt. He left Fisk in there with broken ribs and we'd sit there in the bleachers and watch the pitching and we'd say it's time to take him out, but Zimmer would leave him in too long. We've been sitting here in these bleacher seats since 1964. We get here three, four hours before a game. I have been a Red Sox fan for over 30 years, but I thought that Joe Dee had it all over Ted Williams as a player. Coming to Fenway Park in person made me a Red Sox fan. Growing up in Rhode Island I was a Yankee fan. My older brothers made me a Yankee fan. Personally, I think that Steinbrenner buys pennants and that they should not be allowing it for it disrupts the whole league. My opinion of the Red Sox owners is that they wouldn't spend a penny if it kills them. They have the money and they want to hoard it. All through the years it seems the Yankee power of the dollar bill has made the other teams like the Red Sox the underdog. I think the Yankee under pressure seems to always win, but I am still a Red Sox fan.

Leo Carroll, *Pawtucket, R.I.*

CALENDAR

HIGH POINTS IN THE RED SOX–YANKEES RIVALRY
THROUGH THE YEARS

January 5, 1920   The Red Sox sell Babe Ruth to the New York Yankees for $125,000. Red Sox owner Harry Frazee also is given a $350,000 mortgage on Fenway Park by Yankee owner Jacob Ruppert.

January 30, 1923   The Yankees acquire pitcher Herb Pennock from Boston for pitcher George Murray, infielder Norm McMillan and outfielder Camp Skinner. The Red Sox also receive cash from New York.

March 22, 1972 Relief ace Sparky Lyle is traded by the Red Sox to the Yankees for outfielder Danny Cater. Mario Guerrero, a shortstop, also is sent to Boston later as part of the deal.

March 29, 1948 The Yankees and Red Sox play through four hours and two minutes to a 2–2 tie in a spring training game in which 33 players are used.

April 14, 1910 The Red Sox and the Yankees play to a 14-inning, Opening Day 4–4 tie.

April 14, 1947 Pitcher Johnny Murphy is signed by the Sox after his release by the Yankees.

April 14, 1967 Bill Rohr, Boston rookie pitcher, defeats the Yankees, 3–0. Rohr has a no-hitter for 8⅔ innings. He winds up with a one-hitter, yielding a single to Elston Howard.

April 16, 1967 The Yanks trim the Sox, 7–6, in an 18-inning game at Yankee Stadium. The time of the game is ten minutes shy of six hours.

April 18, 1950 Using five pitchers in one inning, Boston surrenders a nine-run lead and loses to the Yankees, 15–10.

April 20, 1912 Boston defeats New York, 7–6, in 11 innings in the first official American League game at Fenway Park.

April 20, 1939 Ted Williams racks the ball off the 407-foot sign in right-center field at Yankee Stadium and records his first major league hit, a double.

April 20, 1957 Bill Skowron of the Yankees homers at Fenway Park, putting the ball over the center field wall to the right of the flagpole.

April 21, 1958 The Sox strand 13 runners and score just one run in a game against the Yankees at the Stadium.

April 25, 1946   A 12–5 victory over the Yankees triggers a 15-game Red Sox winning streak.

April 26, 1936   In one of the wildest games ever played between the rivals, the Sox score six runs in the bottom of the first inning and the Yankees rally for seven runs in the top of the second inning.

May 6, 1915   Red Sox pitcher Babe Ruth pounds the first home run of his career off Yankee pitcher Jack Warhop at the Polo Grounds.

May 6, 1918   Babe Ruth bats in the sixth position and plays first base. This is his first major league appearance in a nonpitching or pinch-hitting role, and it comes against his former Red Sox teammates.

May 6, 1930   Pitcher Red Ruffing becomes a Yankee. He is traded by the Red Sox for outfielder Cedric Durst. Boston also receives $50,000.

May 9, 1934   Fred Muller, an infielder, and $20,000 are sent by Boston to the Yankees in exchange for Lyn Lary, infielder.

May 10, 1946   Before 64,183, Boston wins its 15th straight game, edging the Yankees, 5–4, at Yankee Stadium. Joe Dee's grand-slam homer drives in all the runs for the Bronx Bombers.

May 11, 1946   A 2–0 Yankee win ends Boston's 15-game winning streak.

May 20, 1976   A fracas at Yankee Stadium results in an arm injury to Bill Lee. It was alleged that Yankee players caused the injury.

May 25, 1941   Lefty Grove of Boston yields a single to Joe DiMaggio and becomes the first pitcher to participate in two of the greatest streaks in baseball history. The single locked Grove into DiMaggio's 56-game hitting streak.

Grove had also given up one of the homers in Babe Ruth's 60-home-run season.

May 30, 1938   Boston's Joe Cronin and New York's Jake Powell battle at Yankee Stadium.

May 30, 1951   Yankee fans are depressed as Mickey Mantle strikes out five straight times. Red Sox fans are impressed as Ted Williams scores from second base on a sacrifice bunt.

June 2, 1935   Six Yankees hit bases-empty home runs against the Sox.

June 5, 1932   The Yankees acquire Boston pitcher Dan MacFayden for two pitchers and $50,000.

June 17, 1977   Catfish Hunter is pounded for first-inning home runs by Rick Burleson, Fred Lynn, Carlton Fisk and George Scott.

June 18, 1977   Fenway Park is jammed with the largest Saturday afternoon crowd (34,603) in two decades. The crowd is delighted as the Sox trim the Yankees, 10–4. Boston pounds out five home runs.

June 19, 1977   An 11–1 rout gives Boston a three-game series sweep over the Yankees. The Red Sox outhomer New York, 16–0, in the three games as five different Boston players homer in this game.

June 21, 1916   Boston pitcher George Foster hurls a 2–0 no-hitter at Fenway Park against the Yankees.

June 24, 1977   A 6–5 New York win at the Stadium breaks a seven-game Boston winning streak. Three Red Sox homers set a major league record of 33 home runs in ten straight games.

June 26, 1943   Tex Hughson of Boston defeats the Yankees for the eighth straight time.

June 28, 1919   Carl Mays of the Red Sox pitches two

complete games against the Yankees. He wins the first game, 2–0, and is defeated, 4–1, in the second game.

June 28, 1949 A Red Sox–Yankee night game at Fenway draws 36,218 to set a night-game attendance record.

June 29, 1949 Boston's Dom DiMaggio, bidding to break his brother Joe's record, has his consecutive-game hitting streak stopped at 34.

June 30, 1949 Joe DiMaggio completes one of the best series he ever performed in, winding up with four home runs and a single against Boston.

July 1, 1941 A single by Joe DiMaggio enables him to tie Wee Willie Keeler's 44-game hitting streak. DiMaggio's hit comes at Yankee Stadium off Boston pitcher Jack Wilson.

July 2, 1949 Joe DiMaggio sets a new major league record by hitting in his 45th straight game. The hit is a home run off Sox pitcher Heber Newsome.

July 4, 1955 Boston pitchers strike out four Yankee pinch hitters.

July 5, 1937 Joe DiMaggio hits his first grand-slam home run, off Boston pitcher Rube Walberg.

July 5, 1958 The Sox and Yankees play a 3–3, ten-inning tie. The night game takes three hours and 59 minutes to play.

July 7, 1946 New England is in a festive mood as the Sox lead the Yankees by 7½ games in the standings at the All-Star break.

July 8, 1951 A Yankee pitcher fails to complete a game for the 20th consecutive time at Fenway Park.

July 9, 1939 A 4–3 victory over the Yankees gives the Red Sox a sweep of a five-game series and their 12th win in a row.

July 11, 1959 A tenth-inning grand-slam home run by Boston's Don Buddin defeats the Yankees, 8–4.

July 13, 1959 Four days and 20 years after their historic 1939 five-game sweep of the Yankees, the Red Sox do it again. A highlight of Boston's 13–3 pounding of the New Yorkers is a grand-slam home run by Gene Stephens. Inserted as a pinch runner for Ted Williams, he comes to bat when Boston bats around.

July 19, 1978 The Yankees trail Boston by 14 games in the standings.

July 24, 1922 The Red Sox trade Jumping Joe Dugan, third baseman, and Elmer Smith, outfielder, to the Yankees. Outfielders Chick Fewster and Elmer Miller plus shortstop John Miller go to Boston. Much controversy results from the trade, since the Yankees and St. Louis Browns are engaged in a tough pennant race. St. Louis fans claim the trade was too one-sided in favor of the Yankees. The trade leads to the Judge Landis decision that no deals aside from the waiver type could be made after June 15.

July 27, 1975 In the odd setting of Shea Stadium (Yankee Stadium is being refurbished) Red Sox outfielder Fred Lynn's running and stumbling catch ensures a Boston win in the first game of a doubleheader against the Yankees. The Red Sox victory closes out Yankee pennant hopes and Bill Virdon's future as Yankee manager.

July 29, 1919 Boston pitching star Carl Mays is traded to the Yankees for two pitchers and $40,000.

August 1, 1973 Red Sox catcher Carlton Fisk and Yankee catcher Thurman Munson battle at Fenway Park. The fight is triggered when Munson rams into Fisk at home plate attempting to score from third base on a missed bunt attempt. The winner of the battle is still in dispute, but the Red Sox won the game, 3–2.

August 3, 1967   Yankee catcher Elston Howard is acquired by the Red Sox.

August 12, 1934   Babe Ruth's final appearance at Fenway Park draws 41,766 fans to honor the former Sox star.

August 29, 1967   Boston ekes out a 4–3, 20-inning victory over the Yankees in the second game of a twinight doubleheader.

September 3, 1947   The Yankees notch 18 singles against the Red Sox in a game played at Fenway.

September 5, 1927   The final home run hit by Babe Ruth at the Polo Grounds is given up by Boston's Herb Pennock. On May 1, 1920, Pennock had served up Ruth's first Polo Grounds' round tripper.

September 5, 1927   The Sox outlast the Yankees, 12–11, in an 18-inning marathon at Fenway Park.

September 6, 1954   Ten Yankee pinch hitters are used against the Sox.

September 8, 1937   The Yankees score eight times in the ninth inning with two out and defeat Boston, 9–6.

September 9, 1974   A 6–3 Yankee win over the Red Sox is their first victory at Fenway since July 31, 1973.

September 10, 1978   For the first time in ten years, the Sox are swept in a four-game series at Fenway. The 7–4 win moves the Yankees into a first-place tie with Boston.

September 12, 1979   Carl Yastrzemski records the 3,000th hit of his career in a game against the Yankees.

September 21, 1956   Mickey Mantle slugs a home run into the center-field bleachers off Sox pitcher Frank Sullivan. The tape-measure homer barely misses clearing the wall.

September 22, 1955   Fenway Park is so crowded that 5,000 fans are located in the outfield for a Yankee-Sox contest.

September 24, 1919   Babe Ruth's 28th home run sets a major league single-season record. The home run comes off New York's Bob Shawkey.

September 24, 1949   The surging Red Sox defeat the Yankees, 4–1, to move into a tie with New York for first place. Boston had trailed the Bronx Bombers by a dozen games on the Fourth of July.

September 25, 1949   Yankee and Red Sox fans devote a moment of silent prayer to the memory of former New York manager Miller Huggins, who died earlier in the day.

September 27, 1923   Lou Gehrig records his first major league home run, hitting one at Fenway Park off Boston pitcher Bill Piercy.

September 27, 1975   Two Yankee wins over Baltimore enable the Red Sox to clinch the pennant.

September 28, 1923   The Yankees wallop the Sox, 24–4. Boston pitcher Howard Ehmke is pounded for 21 hits and 17 runs in six innings.

September 28, 1951   New York's Allie Reynolds pitches a pennant clinching no-hitter against the Red Sox, giving the Yankees an 8–0 victory.

September 28, 1977   Tiny Fenway Park draws its two millionth fan of the season. The Red Sox go over the two-million mark for the first time ever and become the fourth club in the American League to break that attendance plateau.

October 1, 1961 Roger Maris pounds his record-breaking 61st home run of the season. The historic home run is hit at Yankee Stadium off Boston Red Sox pitcher Tracy Stallard.

October 2, 1949 A 5–3 Yankee win over Boston gives them the pennant and drops the Sox into another runnerup finish on the final day of the season.

October 2, 1978 Bucky Dent's three-run home run helps the Yankees defeat Boston, 5–4, in the second single-game play-off in American League history.

October 3, 1948 A 10–5 Boston win over the Yankees enables the Sox to tie Cleveland for the pennant and move into the first single-game play-off in American League history.

October 28, 1920 Ed Barrow leaves Boston to become the business manager of the New York Yankees.

November 22, 1957 Mickey Mantle is named American League Most Valuable Player, angering Red Sox fans who thought that Ted Williams should have won the award.

December 15, 1920 Boston trades pitchers Waite Hoyt and Harry Harper, infielder Mike McNally and catcher Wally Schang to the Yankees. The Sox receive outfielder Sam Vick, third baseman Derrill Pratt, pitcher Herb Thormahlen, catcher Muddy Ruel and cash.

December 20, 1921 Boston trades pitchers Joe Bush and Sam Jones and shortstop Everett Scott to the Yankees for three pitchers, shortstop Roger Peckinpaugh and cash.

December 21, 1918 Boston sends pitchers Ernie Shore and Dutch Leonard and outfielder Duffy Lewis to the Yankees for four second-line players and cash.

STATS

FINAL POSITIONS IN STANDINGS, 1901–1981

YEAR	RED SOX	YANKEES	YEAR	RED SOX	YANKEES
1901	2		1911	5	6
1902	3		1912	1	8
1903	1	4	1913	4	7
1904	1	2	1914	2	6 (tie)
1905	4	6	1915	1	5
1906	8	2	1916	1	4
1907	7	5	1917	2	6
1908	5	8	1918	1	4
1909	3	5	1919	6	3
1910	4	2	1920	5	3

YEAR	RED SOX	YANKEES	YEAR	RED SOX	YANKEES
1921	5	1	1952	6	1
1922	8	1	1953	4	1
1923	8	1	1954	4	2
1924	7	2	1955	4	1
1925	8	7	1956	4	1
1926	8	1	1957	3	1
1927	8	1	1958	3	1
1928	8	1	1959	5	3
1929	8	2	1960	7	1
1930	8	3	1961	6	1
1931	6	2	1962	8	1
1932	8	1	1963	7	1
1933	7	2	1964	8	1
1934	4	2	1965	9	6
1935	4	2	1966	9	10
1936	6	1	1967	1	9
1937	5	1	1968	4	5
1938	2	1	1969	3	5
1939	2	1	1970	3	2
1940	4	3	1971	3	4
1941	2	1	1972	2	4
1942	2	1	1973	2	4
1943	7	1	1974	3	2
1944	4	3	1975	1	3
1945	7	4	1976	3	1
1946	1	3	1977	2	1
1947	3	1	1978	2	1
1948	2	3	1979	3	4
1949	2	1	1980	4	1
1950	3	1	1981	5	1 (1st half)
1951	3	1		**2	5 (2nd half)

** Tied for second place

JOSEPH PAUL (*Yankee Clipper*) DI MAGGIO

Born November 25, 1914, at Martinez, Calif. Height, 6.02. Weight, 193. Threw and batted righthanded. Brother Dominic with Boston Red Sox, 1940 to spring of 1953, brother Vincent with Boston Braves, 1937–38; Cincinnati Reds, 1939–40; Pittsburgh Pirates, 1940 through 1944; Philadelphia Phillies, 1945–46 and New York Giants, 1946.

Hit safely in 61 consecutive games with San Francisco, Pacific Coast League, 1933; made 206 safe hits in his first complete season with New York Yankees (1936); equaled modern major and American League record for most three-base hits, game (3), first game, August 27, 1938; made two home runs, fifth inning, June 24, 1936; hit three home runs in a game, second game, June 13, 1937, May 23, 1948 and September 10, 1950; first player to hit three home runs in a game at Griffith Stadium, September 10, 1950; hit for cycle, July 9, 1937 and May 20, 1948; batted safely in 56 consecutive games before being stopped by pitchers Al Smith and Jim Bagby of Cleveland in a night game, July 17, 1941, for a major league record; led American League in hit by pitcher (8), 1948; led in total bases, 1937–41–48; tied American League record for fielding percentage by outfielder held by Milt Byrnes of Browns, 1947, and broken by Walter Evers of Detroit in 1950.

World Series record—Co-holder, most times at bat, game (6), October 6, 1936; most times at bat, inning (2), ninth inning, October 6, 1936 and sixth inning, October 6, 1937; most hits, inning (2), ninth inning, October 6, 1936; most putouts, inning (3), ninth inning, October 2, 1936 and sixth inning, October 7, 1937; hit safely in every game of 1939 Series (4 games); holds record for most putouts, one Series, five games (20), 1942.

Named Most Valuable Player, American League, 1939, 1941 and 1947. Named by Baseball Writers' Association of America for THE SPORTING NEWS All-Star Major League Teams, 1937–38–39–40–41–42–47–48. Topped the poll from 1937 to 1941, being unanimous choice in 1939 and 1941. Named by THE SPORTING NEWS as the No. 1 Major League Player of the year, 1939.

Executive vice-president-coach, Oakland Athletics, 1968.

Named to Hall of Fame, 1955.

Year	Club	League	Pos.	G.	AB.	R.	H.	2B.	3B.	HR.	RBI.	B.A.	PO.	A.	E.	F.A.
1932—San Francisco	P. C.	OF	3	9	2	2	1	1	0	2	.222	4	7	1	.917
1933—San Francisco	P. C.	OF	187	762	129	259	45	13	28	*169	.340	407	*32	17	.963
1934—San Francisco	P. C.	OF	101	375	58	128	18	6	12	69	.341	236	11	8	.969
1935—San Francisco	P. C.	OF	172	679	173	270	48	18	34	*154	.398	430	*32	21	.957
1936—New York	Amer.	OF	138	637	132	206	44	*15	29	125	.323	339	*22	8	.978
1937—New York	Amer.	OF	151	621	*151	215	35	15	*46	167	.346	*413	21	*17	.962
1938—New York	Amer.	OF	145	599	129	194	32	13	32	140	.324	366	20	15	.963
1939—New York	Amer.	OF	120	462	108	176	32	6	30	126	*.381	328	13	5	.986
1940—New York	Amer.	OF	132	508	93	179	28	9	31	133	*.352	359	5	8	.978
1941—New York	Amer.	OF	139	541	122	193	43	11	30	*125	.357	385	16	9	.978
1942—New York	Amer.	OF	154	610	123	186	29	13	21	114	.305	409	10	8	.981
1943-44-45—New York	Amer.					(In Military Service)										
1946—New York	Amer.	OF	132	503	81	146	20	8	25	95	.290	314	15	6	.982
1947—New York	Amer.	OF	141	534	97	168	31	10	20	97	.315	316	2	1	*.997
1948—New York	Amer.	OF	153	594	110	190	26	11	*39	*155	.320	441	8	13	.972
1949—New York	Amer.	OF	76	272	58	94	14	6	14	67	.346	195	1	3	.985
1950—New York	Amer.	OF	139	525	114	158	33	10	32	122	.301	376	9	9	.977
1951—New York	Amer.	OF	116	415	72	109	22	4	12	71	.263	283	11	3	.990
Major League Totals			1736	6821	1390	2214	389	131	361	1537	.325	4529	153	105	.978.

WORLD SERIES RECORD

Year	Club	League	Pos.	G.	AB.	R.	H.	2B.	3B.	HR.	RBI.	B.A.	PO.	A.	E.	F.A.
1936—New York	Amer.	OF	6	26	3	9	3	0	0	3	.346	18	0	1	.947
1937—New York	Amer.	OF	5	22	2	6	0	0	1	4	.273	18	0	0	1.000
1938—New York	Amer.	OF	4	15	4	4	0	0	1	2	.267	10	0	0	1.000
1939—New York	Amer.	OF	4	16	3	5	0	0	1	3	.313	11	0	0	1.000
1941—New York	Amer.	OF	5	19	1	5	0	0	0	1	.263	19	0	0	1.000
1942—New York	Amer.	OF	5	21	3	7	0	0	0	3	.333	20	0	0	1.000
1947—New York	Amer.	OF	7	26	4	6	0	0	2	5	.231	22	0	0	1.000
1949—New York	Amer.	OF	5	18	2	2	0	0	1	2	.111	7	0	0	1.000
1950—New York	Amer.	OF	4	13	2	4	1	0	1	2	.308	8	0	0	1.000
1951—New York	Amer.	OF	6	23	3	6	2	0	1	5	.261	17	0	0	1.000
World Series Totals			51	199	27	54	6	0	8	30	.271	150	0	1	.993

THEODORE SAMUEL (*The Kid*) WILLIAMS

Born August 30, 1918, at San Diego, Calif. Height, 6.04. Weight, 198. Threw right and batted lefthanded.

Led American League in 1941 with .406 batting average to become the first major leaguer to hit .400 or more in a decade. In winning his fifth batting crown in 1957, Ted at 39 years of age became the oldest player in the history of the majors to win a batting crown, won again at 40 in '58.

Holds major league record for most consecutive playing years leading in runs scored (5). 1940–41–42–46–47 (in military service, 1943–44–45); also holds major league mark for most consecutive playing years leading in bases on balls (6), 1941–42–46–47–48–49 during the six-year span previously listed. Williams received 100 or more bases on balls each season, establishing record for most consecutive playing years 100 or more bases on balls.

While George Herman (Babe) Ruth is unofficially credited with as many as 80 intentional bases on balls in a season, Ted Williams holds the official record for most intentional bases on balls, season (33), 1957.

Holds major league mark for most successive times reaching first base safely (16). September 17 (hit homer as pinch-hitter), September 13 (walked as pinch-hitter), September 20 (hit homer as pinch-hitter), September 21 (homer and three bases on balls), September 22 (homer, single and three bases on balls), September 23 (single, three bases on balls and hit by pitcher)—1957.

Tied major league record by hitting three home runs in a game twice during 1957 season, May 8 and June 13, 1957; also hit three home runs in a game July 14, 1946 (first game); tied major league record for most home runs in consecutive times at bat (4), September 17–20–21–22, 1957. (Bases on balls received in this span do not count against "consecutive" mark.)

Tied American League record for most total bases in fewest consecutive times at bat (22), September 17–20–21–22–23–24, 1957 (first two times at bat). Eight at-bats, five home runs—a percentage of .275 bases per at-bat. Led in total bases, 1939–42–46–47–49–51; led in bases on balls, 1941–42–46–47–48–49–51–54; led in slugging percentage, 1941–42–46–47–48–49–51–54–54–57; led outfielders in double plays, 1951.

Hit for cycle, second game, July 21, 1946; had lifetime slugging percentage of .645. Hit home run on last at-bat in career, September 28, 1960.

Named Most Valuable Player in American League, 1946-49, and lost to Joe DiMaggio of New York Yankees by one point in 1947.

Named as outfielder on The Sporting News All-Star Major League teams, 1939-40-41-42-46-47-48-49-51-53-55-56-57-58.

Named Top American League Player by The Sporting News, 1957.

Named Major League Player of the Year by The Sporting News, 1941-42-47-49-57.

Named to Hall of Fame, 1966.

Year	Club	League	Pos	G.	AB.	R.	H.	2B.	3B.	HR.	RBI.	B.A.	PO.	A.	E.	F.A.
1936—San Diego	P. C.		OF	42	107	18	29	8	2	0	11	.271	64	5	2	.972
1937—San Diego	P. C.		OF	138	454	66	132	24	2	23	98	.291	213	10	7	.970
1938—Minneapolis	A. A.		OF	148	528	*130	193	30	9	*43	*142	.366	269	17	11	.963
1939—Boston	Amer.		OF	149	565	131	185	44	11	31	*145	.327	318	11	*19	.945
1940—Boston	Amer.		OF	144	561	*134	193	43	14	23	113	.344	302	15	13	.961
1941—Boston	Amer.		OF	143	456	*135	185	33	3	*37	120	.406	262	11	11	.961
1942—Boston	Amer.		OF	150	522	*141	186	34	5	*36	*137	.356	313	15	4	.988
1943-44-45—Boston	Amer.		(In Military Service)													
1946—Boston	Amer.		OF	150	514	*142	176	37	8	38	123	.342	325	7	10	.971
1947—Boston	Amer.		OF	156	528	*125	181	40	9	*32	*114	*.343	347	10	9	.975
1948—Boston	Amer.		OF	137	509	124	188	*44	3	25	127	*.369	289	9	5	.983
1949—Boston	Amer.		OF	*155	566	*150	194	*39	3	*43	*159	.343	337	12	6	.983
1950—Boston(a)	Amer.		OF	89	334	82	106	24	1	28	97	.317	165	7	8	.956
1951—Boston	Amer.		OF	148	531	109	169	28	4	30	126	.318	315	12	4	.988

Year	Club	League	Pos.	G.	AB.	R.	H.	2B.	3B.	HR.	RBI.	B.A.	PO.	A.	E.	F.A.
1952—Boston(b)	....	Amer.	OF	6	10	2	4	0	1	1	3	.400	4	0	0	1.000
1953—Boston(b)	....	Amer.	OF	37	91	17	37	6	0	13	34	.407	31	1	1	.970
1954—Boston	....	Amer.	OF	117	386	93	133	23	1	29	89	.345	213	5	4	.982
1955—Boston	....	Amer.	OF	98	320	77	114	21	3	28	83	.356	170	5	2	.989
1956—Boston	....	Amer.	OF	136	400	71	138	28	2	24	82	.345	174	7	5	.973
1957—Boston	....	Amer.	OF	132	420	96	163	28	1	38	87	*.388	215	2	1	.995
1958—Boston	....	Amer.	OF	129	411	81	135	23	2	26	85	*.328	154	3	7	.957
1959—Boston	....	Amer.	OF	103	272	32	69	15	0	10	43	.254	94	4	3	.970
1960—Boston	....	Amer.	OF	113	310	56	98	15	0	29	72	.316	131	6	1	.993
Major League Totals	....			2292	7706	1798	2654	525	71	521	1839	.344	4159	142	113	.974

a Suffered fractured left elbow when he crashed into the left field wall making catch in first inning of All-Star Game at Chicago, July 11, 1950; despite injury he stayed in game until ninth inning. Williams had played 70 American League games up to the All-Star affair—but appeared in only 19 more contests with the Red Sox for the rest of the season.

b In Military Service most of the season.

PITCHING RECORD

Year	Club	League	G.	IP	W.	L.	Pct.	H.	R.	ER.	SO.	BB.	ERA.
1936—San Diego	....	Pacific Coast	1	1⅓	0	0	.000	2	2	2	0	1	13.50
1940—Boston	....	American	1	2	0	0	.000	3	1	1	1	0	4.50

WORLD SERIES RECORD

Year	Club	League	Pos.	G.	AB.	R.	H.	2B.	3B.	HR.	RBI.	B.A.	PO.	A.	E.	F.A.
1946—Boston	....	Amer.	OF	7	25	2	5	0	0	0	1	.200	16	2	0	1.000

BABE RUTH'S 60 HOME RUNS—1927

HR No.	Team game No.	Date.	Opposing Pitcher and Club.	City.	IN.	O.B.
1	4	April 15	Howard J. Ehmke (R), Phila.	New York	1	0
2	11	April 23	George E. Walberg (L), Phila.	Philadelphia	1	0
3	12	April 24	Hollis Thurston (R), Wash.	Washington	6	0
4	14	April 29	Bryan W. Harriss (R), Boston	Boston	5	0
5	16	May 1	John P. Quinn (R), Phila.	New York	1	1
6	16	May 1	George E. Walberg (L), Phila.	New York	8	0
7	24	May 10	Milton Gaston (R), St. Louis	St. Louis	1	2
8	25	May 11	Ernest Nevers (R), St. Louis	St. Louis	1	1
9	29	May 17	H. Warren Collins (R), Detroit	Detroit	8	0
10	33	May 22	Benj. J. Karr (R), Cleveland	Cleveland	6	1
11	34	May 23	Hollis Thurston (R), Wash.	Washington	1	0
12	37	May 28*	Hollis Thurston (R), Wash.	New York	7	2
13	39	May 29	Daniel K. MacFayden (R), Boston	New York	8	0
14	41	May 30‡	George E. Walberg (L), Phila.	Philadelphia	11	0
15	42	May 31*	John P. Quinn (R), Phila.	Philadelphia	1	1
16	43	May 31†	Howard J. Ehmke (R), Phila.	Philadelphia	5	1
17	47	June 5	Earl O. Whitehill (L), Detroit	New York	6	0
18	48	June 7	Alphonse T. Thomas (R), Chi.	New York	4	0
19	52	June 11	Garland M. Buckeye (L), Cleve.	New York	3	1
20	52	June 11	Garland M. Buckeye (L), Cleve.	New York	5	0
21	53	June 12	George E. Uhle (R), Cleveland	New York	7	0

22	55	June 16	Jonathan T. Zachary (L), St. L.	New York	1	1
23	60	June 22*	Harold J. Wiltse (L), Boston	Boston	5	0
24	60	June 22*	Harold J. Wiltse (L), Boston	Boston	7	1
25	70	June 30	Bryan W. Harriss (R), Boston	New York	4	1
26	73	July 3	Horace O. Lisenbee (R), Wash.	Washington	1	0
27	78	July 8†	Earl O. Whitehill (L), Detroit	Detroit	2	2
28	79	July 9*	Kenneth E. Holloway (R), Detroit	Detroit	1	1
29	79	July 9*	Kenneth E. Holloway (R), Detroit	Detroit	4	2
30	83	July 12	Joseph B. Shaute (L), Cleve.	Cleveland	9	1
31	94	July 24	Alphonse T. Thomas (R), Chi.	Chicago	3	0
32	95	July 25*	Milton Gaston (R), St. Louis	New York	1	1
33	95	July 25*	Milton Gaston (R), St. Louis	New York	6	0
34	98	July 28	Walter C. Stewart (L), St. L.	New York	8	1
35	106	Aug. 5	George S. Smith (R), Detroit	New York	8	0
36	110	Aug. 10	Jonathan T. Zachary (L), Wash.	Washington	3	2
37	114	Aug. 16	Alphonse T. Thomas (R), Chi.	Chicago	5	0
38	115	Aug. 17	George W. Connally (R), Chi.	Chicago	11	0
39	118	Aug. 20	J. Walter Miller (L), Cleveland	Cleveland	1	1
40	120	Aug. 22	Joseph B. Shaute (L), Cleve.	Cleveland	6	0
41	124	Aug. 27	Ernest Nevers (R), St. Louis	St. Louis	8	1
42	125	Aug. 28	J. Ernest Wingard (L), St. Louis	St. Louis	1	1
43	127	Aug. 31	Tony Welzer (R), Boston	New York	8	0
44	128	Sept. 2	George E. Walberg (L), Phila.	Philadelphia	1	0
45	132	Sept. 6*	Tony Welzer (R), Boston	Boston	6	2
46	132	Sept. 6*	Tony Welzer (R), Boston	Boston	7	1

HR No.	Team game No.	Date.	Opposing Pitcher and Club.	City.	IN.	O.B.
47	133	Sept. 6†	Jack Russell (R), Boston	Boston	9	0
48	134	Sept. 7	Daniel K. MacFayden (R), Boston	Boston	1	0
49	134	Sept. 7	Bryan W. Harriss (R), Boston	Boston	8	1
50	138	Sept. 11	Milton Gaston (R), St. Louis	New York	4	0
51	139	Sept. 13*	G. Willis Hudlin (R), Cleveland	New York	7	1
52	140	Sept. 13†	Joseph B. Shaute (L), Cleveland	New York	4	0
53	143	Sept. 16	Ted Blankenship (R), Chicago	New York	3	0
54	147	Sept. 18†	Theodore A. Lyons (R), Chicago	New York	5	1
55	148	Sept. 21	Samuel B. Gibson (R), Detroit	New York	9	0
56	149	Sept. 22	Kenneth E. Holloway (R), Detroit	New York	9	1
57	152	Sept. 27	Robert M. Grove (L), Phila.	New York	6	3
58	153	Sept. 29	Horace O. Lisenbee (R), Wash.	New York	1	0
59	153	Sept. 29	Paul Hopkins (R), Washington	New York	5	3
60	154	Sept. 30	Jonathan T. Zachary (L), Wash.	New York	8	1

* First game of double-header.

† Second game of double-header.

‡ Afternoon game.

New York A. L. played 155 games in 1927 (one tie on April 14), with Ruth participating in 151 games.

JOE DIMAGGIO'S 56-GAME HITTING STREAK—1941

Date.	Opp. Pitcher and Club.	AB.	R.	H.	2B.	3B.	HR.	RBI.
May 15	Smith, Chicago	4	0	1	0	0	0	1
16	Lee, Chicago	4	2	2	0	1	1	1
17	Rigney, Chicago	3	1	1	0	0	0	0
18	Harris (2), Niggeling (1), St. Louis	3	3	3	1	0	0	1
19	Galehouse, St. Louis	3	0	1	1	0	0	0
20	Auker, St. Louis	5	1	1	0	0	0	1
21	Rowe (1), Benton (1), Detroit	5	0	2	0	0	0	1
22	McKain, Detroit	4	0	1	0	0	0	1
23	Newsome, Boston	5	0	1	0	0	0	2
24	Johnson, Boston	4	2	1	0	0	0	2
25	Grove, Boston	4	0	1	0	0	0	0
27	Chase (1), Anderson (2), Carrasquel (1), Washington	5	3	4	0	0	1	3
28	Hudson, Washington (Night)	4	1	1	0	1	0	0
29	Sundra, Washington	3	1	1	0	0	0	0
30	Johnson, Boston	2	1	1	0	0	0	0
30	Harris, Boston	3	0	1	1	0	0	0
June 1	Milnar, Cleveland	4	1	1	0	0	0	0
1	Harder, Cleveland	4	0	1	0	0	0	0
2	Feller, Cleveland	4	2	2	1	0	0	0
3	Trout, Detroit	4	1	1	0	0	1	1
5	Newhouser, Detroit	5	1	1	0	1	0	1

Date	Opp. Pitcher and Club	AB.	R.	H.	2B.	3B.	HR.	RBI.
June	7—Muncrief (1), Allen (1), Caster (1), St. Louis	5	2	3	0	0	0	1
	8—Auker, St. Louis	4	3	2	0	0	2	4
	8—Caster (1), Kramer (1), St. Louis	4	1	2	1	0	1	3
	10—Rigney, Chicago	5	1	1	0	0	0	0
	12—Lee, Chicago (Night)	4	1	2	0	0	1	1
	14—Feller, Cleveland	2	0	1	1	0	0	1
	15—Bagby, Cleveland	3	1	1	0	0	1	1
	16—Milnar, Cleveland	5	0	1	1	0	0	0
	17—Rigney, Chicago	4	1	1	0	0	0	0
	18—Lee, Chicago	3	0	1	0	0	0	0
	19—Smith (1), Ross (2), Chicago	3	2	3	0	0	1	2
	20—Newsom (2), McKain (2), Detroit	5	3	4	1	0	0	1
	21—Trout, Detroit	4	0	1	0	0	0	1
	22—Newhouser (1), Newsom (1), Detroit	5	1	2	1	0	1	2
	24—Muncrief, St. Louis	4	1	1	0	0	0	0
	25—Galehouse, St. Louis	4	1	1	0	0	1	3
	26—Auker, St. Louis	4	0	1	1	0	0	1
	27—Dean, Philadelphia	3	1	2	0	0	1	2
	28—Babich (1), Harris (1), Philadelphia	5	1	2	1	0	0	0
	29—Leonard, Washington	4	1	1	1	0	0	0
	29—Anderson, Washington	5	1	1	0	0	0	1

July		AB	R	H				
1—Harris (1), Ryba (1), Boston		4	0	2	0	0	0	1
1—Wilson, Boston		3	1	1	0	0	0	1
2—Newsome, Boston		5	1	1	0	1	1	3
5—Marchildon, Philadelphia		4	2	1	0	1	1	2
6—Babich (1), Hadley (3), Philadelphia		5	2	4	1	0	0	2
6—Knott, Philadelphia		4	0	2	0	0	0	2
10—Niggeling, St. Louis (Night)		2	0	1	0	0	0	0
11—Harris (3), Kramer (1), St. Louis		5	1	4	0	0	1	2
12—Auker (1), Muncrief (1), St. Louis		5	1	2	1	0	0	1
13—Lyons (2), Hallett (1), Chicago		4	2	3	0	0	0	0
13—Lee, Chicago		4	0	1	0	0	0	0
14—Rigney, Chicago		3	0	1	0	0	0	0
15—Smith, Chicago		4	1	2	1	0	0	2
16—Milnar (2), Krakauskas (1), Cleve.		4	3	3	1	0	0	0
Totals For 56 Games		223	56	91	16	4	15	55

BB., 21; SO., 5; HBP., 2.

Stopped July 17 at Cleveland, night game, New York won, 4 to 3. First inning, Alfred J. Smith pitching, thrown out by Keltner; fourth inning, Smith pitching, received base on balls; seventh inning, Smith pitching, thrown out by Keltner; eighth inning, James C. Bagby, Jr., pitching, grounded into double play.

RED SOX YEAR-BY-YEAR

Year	Pos.	W–L	Pct.	GA GB	Manager	Attendance
1981	5 (1st half)	30–26	.536	4	Ralph Houk	[1,060,379
	**2 (2nd half)	29–23	.558	1½	Ralph Houk	total] 1,956,092
1980	4TE	83–77	.519	19	Zimmer–John M. Pesky	2,353,114
1979	3E	91–69	.569	11½	Donald W. Zimmer	2,320,643
1978	2E	99–64	.607	1	Donald W. Zimmer	2,074,549
1977	2TE	97–64	.602	2½	Donald W. Zimmer	1,895,846
1976	3E	83–79	.512	15½	Johnson—Donald W. Zimmer	*1,748,587
1975	1	95–65	.594	4½	Darrell D. Johnson	*1,556,411
1974	3E	84–78	.519	7	Darrell D. Johnson	1,481,002
1973	2E	89–73	.549	8	Edward M. Kasko	1,441,718
1972	2E	85–70	.548	½	Edward M. Kasko	*1,678,732
1971	3E	85–77	.525	18	Edward M. Kasko	*1,595,278
1970	3E	87–75	.537	21	Edward M. Kasko	*1,833,246
1969	3E	87–75	.537	22	Williams—Edward J. Popowski	1,940,788
1968	4	86–76	.531	17	Richard H. Williams	*1,727,832
1967	1	92–70	.568	1	Richard H. Williams	811,172
1966	9	72–90	.444	26	Herman—James E. (Pete) Runnels	652,201
1965	9	62–100	.383	40	William J. Herman	883,276
1964	8	72–90	.444	27	Pesky—William J. Herman	942,642
1963	7	76–85	.472	28	John M. Pesky	

Year	Finish	W–L	GB	Pct	Manager	Attendance
1962	8	76–84	19	.475	Michael F. Higgins	733,080
1961	6	76–86	33	.469	Michael F. Higgins	850,589
1960	7	65–89	32	.422	Jurges—Michael F. Higgins	1,129,866
1959	5	75–79	19	.487	Higgins, R. York, William F. Jurges	984,102
1958	3	79–75	13	.513	Michael F. Higgins	1,077,047
1957	3	82–72	16	.532	Michael F. Higgins	1,181,087
1956	4	84–70	13	.545	Michael F. Higgins	1,137,158
1955	4	84–70	12	.545	Michael F. Higgins	1,203,200
1954	4	69–85	42	.448	Louis Boudreau	931,127
1953	4	84–69	16	.549	Louis Boudreau	1,026,133
1952	6	76–78	19	.494	Louis Boudreau	1,115,750
1951	3	87–67	11	.565	Stephen F. O'Neill	1,312,282
1950	3	94–60	4	.610	McCarthy—Stephen F. O'Neill	1,344,080
1949	2	95–58	1	.623	Joseph V. McCarthy	1,596,650
1948	2	96–59	1	.619	Joseph V. McCarthy	1,558,798
1947	3	83–71	14	.539	Joseph E. Cronin	1,427,315
1946	1	104–50	12	.675	Joseph E. Cronin	1,416,944
1945	7	71–83	17½	.461	Joseph E. Cronin	603,794
1944	4	77–77	12	.500	Joseph E. Cronin	506,975
1943	7	68–84	29	.447	Joseph E. Cronin	358,275
1942	2	93–59	9	.612	Joseph E. Cronin	730,340
1941	2	84–70	17	.545	Joseph E. Cronin	718,497
1940	4	82–72	8	.532	Joseph E. Cronin	716,234

Year	Pos.	W–L	Pct.	GA GB	Manager	Attendance
1939	2	89–62	.589	17	Joseph E. Cronin	573,070
1938	2	88–61	.591	9½	Joseph E. Cronin	646,459
1937	5	80–72	.526	21	Joseph E. Cronin	559,659
1936	6	74–80	.481	28½	Joseph E. Cronin	626,895
1935	4	78–75	.510	16	Joseph E. Cronin	558,568
1934	4	76–76	.500	24	Stanley R. (Bucky) Harris	610,640
1933	7	63–86	.423	34½	Martin J. McManus	268,715
1932	8	43–111	.279	64	Collins—Martin J. McManus	182,150
1931	6	62–90	.408	45	John F. (Shano) Collins	350,975
1930	8	52–102	.338	50	Charles H. Wagner	444,045
1929	8	58–96	.377	48	William F. Carrigan	394,620
1928	8	57–96	.373	43½	William F. Carrigan	396,920
1927	8	51–103	.331	59	William F. Carrigan	305,275
1926	8	46–107	.301	44½	Lee A. Fohl	285,155
1925	8	47–105	.309	49½	Lee A. Fohl	267,782
1924	7	67–87	.435	25	Lee A. Fohl	448,556
1923	8	61–91	.401	37	Frank L. Chance	229,668
1922	8	61–93	.396	33	Hugh Duffy	259,184
1921	5	75–79	.487	23½	Hugh Duffy	279,273
1920	5	72–81	.471	25½	Edward G. Barrow	402,445
1919	6	66–71	.482	20½	Edward G. Barrow	417,291
1918	1	75–51	.595	2½	Edward G. Barrow	249,513
1917	2	90–62	.592	9	John J. Barry	387,856
1916	1	91–63	.591	2	William F. Carrigan	496,397

Year		Record	Pct.	GB	Manager	Attendance
1915	1	101–50	.669	2½	William F. Carrigan	539,885
1914	2	91–62	.595	8½	William F. Carrigan	481,359
1913	4	79–71	.527	15½	Stahl—William F. Carrigan	437,194
1912	1	105–47	.691	14	J. Garland (Jake) Stahl	597,096
1911	5	78–75	.510	24	Patrick J. Donovan	503,961
1910	4	81–72	.529	22½	Patrick J. Donovan	584,619
1909	3	88–63	.583	9½	Fred Lake	668,965
1908	5	75–79	.487	15½	McGuire—Fred Lake	473,048
1907	7	59–90	.396	32½	George Huff—Bob Unglaub—Cy Young, James McGuire	436,777
1906	8	49–105	.318	45½	Collins—Charles S. Stahl	410,209
1905	4	78–74	.513	16	James J. Collins	468,828
1904	1	95–59	.617	1½	James J. Collins	623,295
1903	1	91–47	.659	14½	James J. Collins	379,338
1902	3	77–60	.562	6½	James J. Collins	348,567
1901	2	79–57	.581	4	James J. Collins	289,448

*Led league
** Tied for second place

RED SOX IN WORLD SERIES

Year	Opp	Winner	Games	Year	Opp	Winner	Games
1903	Pitt.	Bos.	5–3	1918	Chi.	Bos.	4–2
1904	no series held			1946	St. L.	St. L.	4–3
1912	N.Y.	Bos.	4–3–1	1967	St. L.	St. L.	4–3
1915	Phil.	Bos.	4–1	1975	Cinn.	Cinn.	4–3
1916	Brook.	Bos.	4–1				

NEW YORK YANKEES—YEAR-BY-YEAR

Year	Position	Won	Lost	Pct.	Manager	Attendance
1903	Fourth	72	62	.537	Clark Griffith	211,808
1904	Second	92	59	.609	Clark Griffith	438,919
1905	Sixth	71	78	.477	Clark Griffith	309,100
1906	Second	90	61	.596	Clark Griffith	434,700
1907	Fifth	70	78	.473	Clark Griffith	350,020
1908	Eighth	51	103	.331	Griffith-N. Elberfeld	305,500
1909	Fifth	74	77	.490	George T. Stallings	501,000
1910	Second	88	63	.583	Stallings-Hal Chase	355,857
1911	Sixth	76	76	.500	Hal Chase	302,444
1912	Eighth	50	102	.329	Harry Wolverton	242,194
1913	Seventh	57	94	.377	Frank Chance	357,551
1914	†Sixth	70	84	.455	Chance-R. Peckinpaugh	359,477
1915	Fifth	69	83	.454	William E. Donovan	256,035
1916	Fourth	80	74	.519	William E. Donovan	469,211
1917	Sixth	71	82	.464	William E. Donovan	330,294
1918	Fourth	60	63	.488	Miller J. Huggins	282,047
1919	Third	80	59	.576	Miller J. Huggins	619,164
1920	Third	95	59	.617	Miller J. Huggins	1,289,422
1921	First	98	55	.641	Miller J. Huggins	1,230,696
1922	First	94	60	.610	Miller J. Huggins	1,026,134
1923	‡First	98	54	.645	Miller J. Huggins	1,007,066

Year	Position	W	L	Pct	Manager	Attendance
1924	Second	89	63	.586	Miller J. Huggins	1,053,533
1925	Seventh	69	85	.448	Miller J. Huggins	697,267
1926	First	91	63	.591	Miller J. Huggins	1,027,095
1927	‡First	110	44	.714	Miller J. Huggins	1,164,015
1928	‡First	101	53	.656	Miller J. Huggins	1,072,132
1929	Second	88	66	.571	Huggins-Fletcher	960,148
1930	Third	86	68	.558	Robert Shawkey	1,169,230
1931	Second	94	59	.614	Joe McCarthy	912,437
1932	Second	107	47	.695	Joe McCarthy	962,320
1933	‡First	91	59	.607	Joe McCarthy	728,014
1934	Second	94	60	.610	Joe McCarthy	854,682
1935	Second	89	60	.597	Joe McCarthy	657,508
1936	‡First	102	51	.667	Joe McCarthy	976,913
1937	‡First	102	52	.662	Joe McCarthy	998,148
1938	‡First	99	53	.651	Joe McCarthy	970,916
1939	‡First	106	45	.702	Joe McCarthy	859,785
1940	Third	88	66	.571	Joe McCarthy	988,975
1941	‡First	101	53	.656	Joe McCarthy	964,722
1942	First	103	51	.669	Joe McCarthy	988,251
1943	‡First	98	56	.636	Joe McCarthy	645,006
1944	Third	83	71	.539	Joe McCarthy	822,864
1945	Fourth	81	71	.553	Joe McCarthy	881,846
1946	Third	87	67	.565	McCarthy-W. Dickey-Neun	2,265,512

Year	Position	Won	Lost	Pct.	Manager	Attendance
1947	‡First	97	57	.630	Bucky Harris	2,178,937
1948	Third	94	60	.610	Bucky Harris	2,373,901
1949	‡First	97	57	.630	Casey Stengel	2,281,676
1950	‡First	98	56	.636	Casey Stengel	2,081,380
1951	‡First	98	56	.636	Casey Stengel	1,950,107
1952	‡First	95	59	.617	Casey Stengel	1,629,665
1953	‡First	99	52	.656	Casey Stengel	1,537,811
1954	Second	103	51	.669	Casey Stengel	1,475,171
1955	First	96	58	.623	Casey Stengel	1,490,138
1956	‡First	97	57	.680	Casey Stengel	1,491,784
1957	First	98	56	.636	Casey Stengel	1,497,134
1958	‡First	92	62	.597	Casey Stengel	1,428,438
1959	Third	79	75	.513	Casey Stengel	1,552,030
1960	First	97	57	.630	Casey Stengel	1,627,349
1961	‡First	109	53	.673	Ralph Houk	1,747,736
1962	‡First	96	66	.593	Ralph Houk	1,493,574
1963	First	104	57	.646	Ralph Houk	1,308,920
1964	First	99	63	.611	Yogi Berra	1,305,638
1965	Sixth	77	85	.475	Johnny Keane	1,213,552
1966	Tenth	70	89	.440	Keane-Houk	1,124,648
1967	Ninth	72	90	.444	Ralph Houk	1,141,714
1968	Fifth	83	79	.512	Ralph Houk	1,125,124

Year	Finish	W	L	Pct	Manager	Attendance
1969	Fifth	80	81	.497	Ralph Houk	1,067,996
1970	Second	93	69	.574	Ralph Houk	1,136,879
1971	Fourth	82	80	.506	Ralph Houk	1,070,771
1972	Fourth	79	76	.510	Ralph Houk	966,328
1973	Fourth	80	82	.494	Ralph Houk	1,262,077
1974	Second	89	73	.549	Bill Virdon	1,273,075
1975	Third	83	77	.519	Virdon-Martin	1,288,048
1976	First	97	62	.610	Billy Martin	2,012,434
1977	‡First	100	62	.617	Billy Martin	2,103,092
1978	‡First	100	63	.613	Martin-Lemon	2,335,871
1979	Fourth	89	71	.556	Lemon-Martin	2,537,765
1980	First	103	59	.636	Dick Howser	2,627,417
1981	First (1st half)	34	22	.607	Gene Michael, Bob Lemon	⎡ 1,614,353
1981	Fifth (2nd half)	25	26	.490	Gene Michael, Bob Lemon	⎣ total

World Champions—22; American League Champions—32

Finished First—33; Second—12; Third—9; Fourth—8; Fifth—5; Sixth—5; Seventh—2; Eighth—2; Ninth—1; Tenth—1.

Highest Percentage—.714 in 1927; Lowest—.329 in 1912.

† Tied with Chicago.
‡ World Championship.

YANKEES IN WORLD SERIES

Year	Won	Lost	Pct.	Games Won By	Manager	World Series Opp	Games Record W.	L.
1921	98	55	.641	4½	Miller Huggins	Giants	3	5
1922	94	60	.610	1	Miller Huggins	Giants	**0	4
*1923	98	54	.645	16	Miller Huggins	Giants	4	2
1926	91	63	.591	3	Miller Huggins	Cardinals	3	4
*1927	110	44	.714	19	Miller Huggins	Pirates	4	0
*1928	101	53	.656	2½	Miller Huggins	Cardinals	4	0
*1932	107	47	.695	13	Joe McCarthy	Cubs	4	0
*1936	102	51	.667	19½	Joe McCarthy	Giants	4	2
*1937	102	52	.662	13	Joe McCarthy	Giants	4	1
*1938	99	53	.651	9½	Joe McCarthy	Cubs	4	0
*1939	106	45	.702	17	Joe McCarthy	Reds	4	0
*1941	101	53	.656	17	Joe McCarthy	Dodgers	4	1
1942	103	51	.669	9	Joe McCarthy	Cardinals	1	4
*1943	98	56	.636	13½	Joe McCarthy	Cardinals	4	1
*1947	97	57	.630	12	Bucky Harris	Dodgers	4	3

Year	W	L	Pct	GB	Manager	Opponent		
*1949	97	57	.630	1	Casey Stengel	Dodgers	4	1
*1950	98	56	.636	3	Casey Stengel	Phillies	4	0
*1951	98	56	.636	5	Casey Stengel	Giants	4	2
*1952	95	59	.617	2	Casey Stengel	Dodgers	4	3
*1953	99	52	.656	8½	Casey Stengel	Dodgers	4	2
1955	96	58	.623	3	Casey Stengel	Dodgers	3	4
*1956	97	57	.630	9	Casey Stengel	Dodgers	4	3
1957	98	56	.636	8	Casey Stengel	Braves	3	4
*1958	92	62	.597	10	Casey Stengel	Braves	4	3
1960	97	57	.630	8	Casey Stengel	Pirates	3	4
*1961	109	53	.673	8	Ralph Houk	Reds	4	1
*1962	96	66	.593	5	Ralph Houk	Giants	4	3
1963	104	57	.646	10½	Ralph Houk	Dodgers	0	4
1964	99	63	.611	1	Yogi Berra	Cardinals	3	4
1976	97	62	.610	10½	Billy Martin	Reds	0	4
*1977	100	62	.617	2½	Billy Martin	Dodgers	4	2
*1978	100	63	.613	1	Billy Martin	Dodgers	4	2
					Bob Lemon			

*World Champions   **Tie game in 1922

ALL-TIME YANKEES—TOP 20 HITTING CATEGORIES

	Games	At Bats	Runs	Hits
1.	Mantle 2401	Mantle 8102	Ruth 1959	Gehrig 2721
2.	Gehrig 2164	Gehrig 8001	Gehrig 1888	Ruth 2518
3.	Berra 2116	Berra 7546	Mantle 1677	Mantle 2415
4.	Ruth 2084	Ruth 7217	DiMaggio 1390	DiMaggio 2214
5.	White 1881	DiMaggio 6821	Combs 1186	Berra 2148
6.	Dickey 1789	White 6650	Berra 1174	Dickey 1969
7.	DiMaggio 1736	Dickey 6300	Crosetti 1006	Combs 1866
8.	Crosetti 1682	Crosetti 6277	White 964	White 1803
9.	Rizzuto 1661	Lazzeri 6094	Lazzeri 952	Lazzeri 1784
10.	Lazzeri 1659	Rizzuto 5816	Rolfe 942	Rizzuto 1588
11.	Howard 1492	Combs 5748	Dickey 930	Pipp 1577
12.	Pipp 1488	Pipp 5594	Henrich 901	Meusel 1565
13.	Combs 1455	Richardson 5386	Rizzuto 877	Munson 1558
14.	Munson 1423	Munson 5344	Pipp 820	Crosetti 1541
15.	Richardson 1412	Howard 5044	Bauer 792	Richardson 1432
16.	Bauer 1406	Meusel 5032	Meusel 764	Howard 1405
17.	McDougald 1336	Rolfe 4827	Keller 714	Rolfe 1394
18.	Meusel 1294	Bauer 4784	McDougald 697	Bauer 1326
19.	Henrich 1284	Clarke 4723	Munson 696	Henrich 1297
20.	Clarke 1230	McDougald 4676	Peckinpaugh 670	McDougald 1291

	Doubles	Triples	Home Runs	RBIs
1.	Gehrig 535	Gehrig 162	Ruth 659	Gehrig 1991
2.	Ruth 424	Combs 154	Mantle 536	Ruth 1970
3.	DiMaggio 389	DiMaggio 131	Gehrig 493	DiMaggio 1537
4.	Mantle 344	Pipp 121	DiMaggio 361	Mantle 1509
5.	Dickey 343	Lazzeri 115	Berra 358	Berra 1430
6.	Meusel 338	Ruth 106	Maris 203	Dickey 1209
7.	Lazzeri 327	Meusel 87	Dickey 202	Lazzeri 1154
8.	Berra 321	Henrich 73	NETTLES 197	Meusel 1005
9.	Combs 309	Mantle 72	Keller 184	Pipp 825
10.	White 300	Dickey 72	Henrich 183	Henrich 795
11.	Henrich 269	Keller 69	Lazzeri 169	White 758
12.	Crosetti 260	Rolfe 67	Pepitone 166	Howard 732
13.	Pipp 259	Stirnweiss 66	Skowron 165	Keller 723
14.	Rolfe 257	Crosetti 65	Howard 161	Munson 701
15.	Rizzuto 239	Chapman 64	MURCER 161	Skowron 672
16.	Munson 229	Rizzuto 62	White 160	NETTLES 658
17.	Howard 211	Cree 62	Bauer 158	Bauer 654
18.	Bauer 211	Conroy 59	Gordon 153	Crosetti 649
19.	Chapman 209	Bauer 56	Meusel 146	MURCER 632
20.	Richardson 196	Peckinpaugh 53	Tresh 140	Combs 629

BATTING AVERAGE
(800 or more games)

1. Ruth .349	6. Meusel .311	11. Lazzeri .293	16. Berra .285
2. Gehrig .340	7. Chapman .305	12. Munson .292	17. Chase .284
3. DiMaggio .325	8. Mantle .298	13. Selkirk .290	18. Pipp .282
4. Combs .325	9. Keeler .295	14. Rolfe .289	19. Henrich .282
5. Dickey .313	10. Skowron .294	15. Keller .285	20. MURCER .281

CAPS—Active Yankee Player

ALL-TIME YANKEES—TOP 20 PITCHING CATEGORIES

	Games	Innings	Wins	Pct. (100 decis.)
1.	498 Ford, W.	3171 Ford, W.	236 Ford, W.	.724 GUIDRY
2.	426 Ruffing	3169 Ruffing	231 Ruffing	.717 Chandler
3.	420 Lyle	2662 Stottlemyre	189 Gomez	.706 Raschi
4.	415 Shawkey	2498 Gomez	168 Shawkey	.690 Ford, W.
5.	383 Murphy	2489 Shawkey	164 Stottlemyre	.686 Reynolds
6.	367 Gomez	2273 Hoyt	162 Pennock	.670 Mays
7.	365 Hoyt	2189 Pennock	157 Hoyt	.657 Lopat
8.	360 Stottlemyre	1953 Chesbro	131 Reynolds	.652 Gomez
9.	346 Pennock	1856 Peterson	126 Chesbro	.651 Ruffing
10.	311 Hamilton	1718 Caldwell	120 Raschi	.643 Pennock
11.	295 Reynolds	1700 Reynolds	113 Lopat	.643 Byrne
12.	288 Peterson	1537 Raschi	109 Peterson	.637 Murphy
13.	278 Page	1497 Lopat	109 Chandler	.616 Hoyt
14.	269 Chesbro	1485 Chandler	96 Caldwell	.612 Bonham
15.	248 Caldwell	1423 Warhop	93 Murphy	.612 Turley
16.	247 Pipgras	1352 Pipgras	93 Pipgras	.595 Pipgras
17.	247 Reniff	1279 Quinn	82 Turley	.577 Chesbro
18.	234 Turley	1268 Turley	79 Mays	.569 Terry
19.	228 Quinn	1236 Downing	79 Bonham	.595 Pipgras
20.	221 Byrne	1198 Terry	78 Terry	.559 Downing

Strikeouts	Shutouts	Complete Games	ERA (Over 800 Inn.)
1. Ford, W.	1956 Ford, W.	45 Ruffing	261 Ford, R. 2.54
2. Ruffing	1526 Stottlemyre	40 Gomez	173 Chesbro 2.58
3. Gomez	1468 Ruffing	40 Chesbro	169 Orth 2.72
4. Stottlemyre	1257 Gomez	28 Pennock	165 GUIDRY 2.73
5. Shawkey	1163 Reynolds	27 Shawkey	161 Bonham 2.73
6. Downing	1028 Chandler	26 Ford, W.	156 Ford, W. 2.74
7. Reynolds	967 Shawkey	24 Hoyt	156 Chandler 2.84
8. Chesbro	913 Raschi	24 Stottlemyre	152 Fisher 2.91
9. Turley	909 Turley	21 Caldwell	151 Stottlemyre 2.99
10. Peterson	893 Lopat	20 Chandler	109 Caldwell 2.99
11. Raschi	832 GUIDRY	19 Warhop	105 Warhop 3.09
12. GUIDRY	818 Pennock	19 Ford, R.	103 Peterson 3.10
13. Caldwell	803 Peterson	18 Orth	102 Shawkey 3.10
14. Hoyt	713 Bonham	17 Raschi	99 Bahnsen 3.10
15. Pennock	656 Chesbro	16 Reynolds	96 Quinn 3.12
16. Pipgras	652 Terry	16 Bonham	91 Lopat 3.25
17. Terry	615 Hoyt	15 Lopat	91 Downing 3.25
18. Chandler	614 Pipgras	13 Pipgras	84 Mays 3.25
19. Byrne	559 Caldwell	13 Quinn	82 Reynolds 3.30
20. Bouton	561 Downing	12 Peterson	81 Gomez 3.34

CAPS—Active Yankee Player

RED SOX ALL-TIME BATTING LEADERS

Home Runs		Runs Batted in		Batting Avg.	
T. Williams	.521	T. Williams	1,839	T. Williams	.344
YASTRZEMSKI	.419	YASTRZEMSKI	1,663	Speaker	.337
Doerr	.223	Doerr	1,247	Foxx	.320
Foxx	.222	Foxx	.788	Runnels	.320
Petrocelli	.210	Petrocelli	.773	R. Johnson	.313
RICE	.196	Cronin	.737	Pesky	.313
Jensen	.170	Jensen	.733	Lynn	.308
FISK	.162	Malzone	.716	RICE	.307
T. Conigliaro	.162	RICE	.669	Goodman	.306
G. Scott	.154	Lewis	.643	Cramer	.302
Smith	.149	D. DiMaggio	.618	R. Ferrell	.302
Malzone	.131			Cronin	.300
EVANS	.128			D. DiMaggio	.298
Lynn	.124				
V. Stephens	.122				

Games

YASTRZEMSKI	2,967
T. Williams	2,292
Doerr	1,865
Hooper	1,646
Petrocelli	1,553
D. DiMaggio	1,399
Malzone	1,359
G. Scott	1,192
Lewis	1,184
Goodman	1,177
Cronin	1,134

At Bats

YASTRZEMSKI	10,811
T. Williams	7,706
Doerr	7,093
Hooper	6,269
D. DiMaggio	5,640
Petrocelli	5,390
Malzone	5,273
Goodman	4,399
Lewis	4,325
G. Scott	4,234
Pesky	4,085

Runs

T. Williams	1,798
YASTRZEMSKI	1,689
Doerr	1,094
D. DiMaggio	1,046
Hooper	988
Pesky	776
Foxx	721
Speaker	703
Goodman	688
Petrocelli	653
Cronin	645

Hits

YASTRZEMSKI	3,109
T. Williams	2,654
Doerr	2,042
Hooper	1,707
D. DiMaggio	1,680
Malzone	1,454
Petrocelli	1,352
Goodman	1,344
Speaker	1,328
Pesky	1,277

Doubles

YASTRZEMSKI	586
T. Williams	525
Doerr	381
D. DiMaggio	308
Cronin	270
Lewis	254
Goodman	248
Hooper	246
Speaker	241
Petrocelli	237
Malzone	234

Triples

Hooper	130
Speaker	106
Freeman	91
Doerr	89
Gardner	87
Ferris	78
T. Williams	71
J. Collins	65
Parent	65
C. Stahl	64

Total Bases		Extra Base Hits		Slugging Pct.	
YASTRZEMSKI	5,066	T. Williams	1,117	T. Williams	.634
T. Williams	4,884	YASTRZEMSKI	1,062	Foxx	.605
Doerr	3,270	Doerr	693	RICE	.545
D. DiMaggio	2,363	Petrocelli	469	Lynn	.520
Hooper	2,303	D. DiMaggio	452	V. Stephens	.492
Petrocelli	2,263	Foxx	448	T. Conigliaro	.488
Malzone	2,123	Cronin	433	Cronin	.484
RICE	1,993	RICE	422	Speaker	.482
Foxx	1,988	Hooper	406	FISK	.481
Speaker	1,898	FISK	402	Jensen	.478
Cronin	1,883	Malzone	386	Smith	.471
FISK	1,856	Smith	386	YASTRZEMSKI	.469
		Speaker	386	Doerr	.461

RED SOX ALL-TIME PITCHING LEADERS

Games		Innings		Games Started	
Kinder	365	Young	2,728	Young	298
Young	327	Tiant	1,774	Tiant	238
Delock	322	Parnell*	1,753	Parnell*	232
Lee*	321	Monbouquette	1,622	Monbouquette	228
Parnell*	289	Winter	1,600	Brewer	217

Formieles	286
Radatz	286
Tiant	274
Lyle*	260
Dobson	259
J. Wilson	258
F. Sullivan	252

Dobson	1,544
Grove*	1,540
Brewer	1,509
F. Sullivan	1,505
Lee*	1,503
Dineen	1,501
Wood	1,416
Hughson	1,376

Dobson	202
F. Sullivan	201
Grove*	189
Nixon	177
Dineen	175
Winter	175
Lee*	167

Wins

Young	193
Parnell*	123
Tiant	122
Wood	116
Dobson	106
Grove*	105
Hughson	96
Monbouquette	96
Lee*	94
Brewer	91
H. Leonard*	90
F. Sullivan	90
Ruth*	89
Kinder	86

Shutouts

Young	39
Wood	28
Tiant	26
H. Leonard*	24
Collins*	20
Parnell*	20
S. Jones	18
Dobson	17
Ruth*	17
Dineen	16
G. Foster	16
Monbouquette	16
Hughson	15

Complete Games

Young	276
Dineen	156
Winter	141
Wood	121
Grove*	119
Parnell*	113
Tiant	113
Ruth*	105
Hughson	99
H. Leonard*	96
Collins*	90
Dobson	90

Losses		Saves		Strikeouts	
Young	112	Radatz	104	Young	1,347
Ruffing	96	Kinder	91	Tiant	1,075
Winter	96	Lyle*	69	Wood	986
Russell	94	Fornieles	48	Monbouquette	969
Monbouquette	91	CAMPBELL	44	F. Sullivan	821
Dineen	86	DRAGO	41	Culp	794
Brewer	82	BURGMEIER	32	Lonborg	784
Tiant	81	Delock	31	H. Leonard*	769
F. Sullivan	80	STANLEY	28	Grove*	743
MacFayden	78	Bolin	28	Brewer	733
Parnell*	75	Kiely*	28	Parnell*	732
		Wyatt	28	E. Wilson	714